♂♂♂♂♂♂♂♂♂♂♂♂♂♂♂

HOW TO "PICK UP" (GET DATES WITH) BEAUTIFUL WOMEN IN NIGHTCLUBS OR ANY OTHER PLACE -SECRETS EVERY MAN SHOULD KNOW-

♀♀♀♀♀♀♀♀♀♀♀♀♀♀♀♀

JOHN EAGAN

EDITORIAL CONSULTANT: LILLIAN EAGAN

Printed in the United States of America

Published by:

Secrets Publishing Inc.
P.O. Box 6312
Freehold, NJ 07728

www.4secret.com

This book is dedicated to my family for their support throughout the years

Thank you V.M.

CONTENTS

Introduction..........ix

Chapter 1
WOMEN IN GENERAL..........1

Chapter 2
PERSUASION..........15

Chapter 3
BODY LANGUAGE..........35

Chapter 4
SECRETS OF BEAUTIFUL WOMEN..........55

Chapter 5
INTERVIEWS WITH 2000
BEAUTIFUL WOMEN..........73

Chapter 6
TOP TEN APPROACHES
GUARANTEED TO WORK..........195

Chapter 7
REJECTION..........209

SUMMARY AND
SUPER TECHNIQUES..........229

QUESTIONS & ANSWERS..........244

**Univers*ity studies included*..........*

♂♂♂♂♂♂♂♂♂♂♂♂♂♂

HOW

TO

"PICK UP"

(GET DATES WITH)

BEAUTIFUL WOMEN

IN NIGHTCLUBS OR ANY OTHER PLACE

-SECRETS EVERY MEN SHOULD KNOW-

♀♀♀♀♀♀♀♀♀♀♀♀♀

INTRODUCTION

Imagine yourself walking into a crowded room, seeing the most beautiful woman in there, and knowing that you have the knowledge and power to have that woman any time you want. This might sound like a fantasy to you, and to many others, but with the proper knowledge and information, which you will get from this book, you will have the know-how to do just that. There is a method and technique to everything in life and this is no different. The idea is to find someone who can unlock the secrets through years of observation and experience and use it to your advantage.

Those beautiful women that send your blood pressure through the roof. The opposite sex that causes feelings inside us men that only we can ever understand. You would have to pump a tanker truck full of testosterone into a female for them to remotely understand the sex drive that we men have to control every day of our lives.

What lies beyond these pages are answers to questions that have baffled men for countless years. The beautiful women that you thought were only something to fantasize about can now become part of your reality. The ones you thought were unreachable will now be within your reach.

There are no tricks involved, there is no magic, no hypnosis, just you properly relating to another individual in the way laid out in this book. Throughout this book, you will learn exactly what the woman is looking for, and expecting, from a man when she is in a nightclub, or any other place for that matter. Exactly how to approach a woman, exactly how to converse with her, what type of attire your should wear, how to groom yourself, how to present yourself, and how to act.

This information was attained from two thousand interviews with beautiful women and over twenty years of hard work. There was no guess work involved with unlocking the secrets that have finally surfaced after all these years. The mystery of what is going on in the minds of these beautiful women can now be revealed.

These women, who were interviewed throughout the years, are all the different personality types you will confront. There are many, and an understanding of these personality types, and what they are looking for, is crucial to the successful pursuit of your dream girl.

You will have my over twenty years of nightclub experience, all in this book, for you to do with what you will. You will have over twenty years of interviews with all types of beautiful women. You will have my over twenty years of observing the male and female species and exactly what their habits are in this relentless pursuit of boy meets girl, which nobody is the master of. But you will be after you read this book. You will have my over twenty years' experience in everything you do wrong, and believe me, 99.9% of the males do everything wrong in the pursuit of the female.

This book will tell you what to do and what not to do. When you are finished reading this book, there won't be any woman out of your reach ever again, and that is something you can't put a price on.

You will learn to detect the subtle body language of females, which seem subtle on the surface, but are neon "come-on" signs to the one who knows how to read them. In this book you will learn how to break the ice. Those crucial first seconds which mean so much when you approach a woman. I will offer a top ten list of opening "pickup lines" which will aid you in this smooth approach. After you have the knowledge, there still may be some anxiety over the possibility of facing rejection, it is a fact of nature. We are all deathly afraid of this rejection which is natural for the human species. But with the knowledge this book offers, you will eliminate your chances of rejection. You will have a better understanding of the anxiety of rejection and what it means to you. You will also know how to psychologically deal with it.

After reading this book, you will be an individual who is confident, charming, and debonair.

Although you may be an average looking guy like me, you can be magnetic and appealing and be able to have any woman you desire at any time.

1

WOMEN IN GENERAL

Let's face some facts, we (men) are barbaric when it comes to sex. For the 100,000 years we've been on this planet, we have been graceless to say the least.

Well, look what we had for role models. The original man carried a bat, hit a female over the head, and dragged her back to the cave by the hair. So, it is understandable that most of us are coarse when we are supposed to be smooth. We are crude when we are supposed to be cultivated. We know nothing of the contemporary standards of correctness when it comes to picking up a beautiful woman.

There was no course to take to learn this stuff. There was no instructional manual to read on how to do this. There was generally just no way for a man to learn the proper methods, until now. The only way for a man to become sophisticated, polished, well bred, and a smooth operator is by reading this book. You won't find it anywhere else.

Before I start, I am going to devote this chapter to giving you information about women in general and what goes on in her psyche.

HOW MEN AND WOMEN THINK

We believe that women are inferior to us and, for the last 100,000 years, women believed it too. We mistook physical body power as being superior throughout the ages, but modern man does not need physical power.

All the power comes from the mind today, so today we are competing on an equal (if not lower) basis. Today's women think a little different now. Women think completely different from the way men think. Just look at the sexual harassment issue. To us men, this is a perfectly natural thing to do. We are the aggressive sex.

We think nothing of commenting about a woman's sexuality right to her face. This is because we as men are the aggressive sex and there would be about one eighth the amount of people on this planet if men did not initiate sex. It comes natural to us, but (and this is a big but) women do not like this type of behavior.

They hate being sexually harassed. To them this is demeaning, degrading, and they feel that they are being belittled by us. This is especially true if you are in the position of power. This makes the female want to scratch your eyes out. However, to us, this is fun. We think women are taking all the fun out of working together. The women, on the other hand, just want to work together in an equal capacity without thre sexual harassment.

This is a purer form of thinking than the way that men think. We as men get up at 7 O'Clock in the morning, and then a minute later we say, "Boy, look at the time. It's seven-o-one and I haven't had sex yet!"

Everything we do is based on sex. We will give up almost anything for it. Look at Marc Antony and Cleopatra for example. Marc was in the middle of a battle when Cleo decided to head back to Egypt. He could care less about the battle, all he wanted was to chase her back to Egypt and have sex, and he did.

HOW WOMEN ARE BRED COMPARED TO MEN

There is an instinctive and natural way about women that men have to understand. The more you understand the female, the more confidence you will have when approaching the female. Knowledge is power, so let's get some background information out of the way so that we can go on.

The woman is bred right from the beginning to be soft, caring, innocent, loving, protecting, and mothering. They are brought up to attend to the wants and comforts of someone. Their first toys are usually baby dolls which they care for and gently handle. They will feed it and rock it and clothe it. They will make it a nice bed and all that. So, what are they being taught from the very beginning? They are being taught to be kind and good and caring to other human beings. Not like us. We get toy tanks and army soldiers, race cars and motorcycles, toy guns, swords, bows, arrows, and everything else that says "get and take what you want in an aggressive manner." Then we grow up watching football and basketball, Robo-Cop and The Terminator which reinforces all that aggressive behavior. Now when we go out to the bar scene, we go out loaded for bear.

WE ARE LIKE ATTILA-THE-HUN SHOPPING AT TIFFANY'S

Women want to nurture and please the right mate.

They are used to giving and don't mind doing it. They also want to get as much as they give. They don't want to be treated badly!

PICKUP VS. ENCOUNTER

She expects a man to have certain social graces. She expects a man to handle the situation in a pleasant manner and to anticipate her wishes. She does not want to feel like she is getting "picked up." You see the word "feel" a lot because women use their feelings and emotions much more than we do. They don't think calculatingly or logically about the meeting. To us it is a "pickup," to them it is meeting an individual with the right qualities to make them happy.

LOOKING FOR LOVE

Ninety-nine percent of the women in lounges have been with men like us. They have been worked over by us unfeeling beings. It's natural for us, but I'm just trying to let you know where they are coming from. This information is power to you. The female thinks entirely different from us. Although they have been worked over many times in their lives, they still think the next one might be "Mr. Right." They are looking for love, their love is unbounding. Once they fall in love, there is nothing they won't do for you.

A woman's love will overpower her personal life such as her career, her family, and all her previous ambitions. All thoughts of matrimony and children fill her head. It is nothing like what we are thinking.

Basically we are shallow and we don't have these thoughts. All we want is sex. Sex with this beautiful woman. And we want it now! We don't usually care about love, honor, marriage, children, or devotion. Our ambitions stay the same no matter what. This is the way men and women are different. They are seeking a complicated emotional fulfillment for themselves and we are seeking a sexual fulfillment.

I'm not saying there is anything wrong with either kind of thinking, I'm just saying it is completely different. When you are going out to pick up a beautiful woman, it helps a great deal to know what is going on in her mind before you make your approach.

I've been trying to help you guys out for over twenty years now. Countless guys come into the lounges I have worked in asking me, "Where's the action," "Who's looking to get picked up" or "who's loose tonight." My reply is, "Every girl in here is available."

THE ATTEMPT TO GET TOGETHER

The truth of the matter is, every girl in a lounge is looking to meet a guy. This is an example of what happens all the time. A guy asks me who the girl is on the other side of the bar. He buys her a drink and then is too afraid to even go over to talk to her. If I only had a nickel for every time this happened, I'd be able to make a nickel plated bra that could fit around the twin towers. This is the fear of rejection which we will discuss in detail later on in the book.

I remember one guy who bought a girl a drink and the girl accepted the drink. She was obviously interested and yet the guy did nothing. After awhile, the girl left and, out of curiosity, I asked the guy why he did not go over to talk with the girl. His reply was simply, "I don't know." I thought it was a shame for both of them because he did not know what to do from that point.

I once had a friend who, because of a car accident, had a little trouble walking. He did not like trying to pickup girls in bars, so he would answer ads in the personal column of the newspaper. He would take out these women who placed the ads and introduce them to me. They were the most horrible looking, fat beasts I ever saw. At that time I thought, "THERE HAS TO BE A BETTER WAY."

Many times I bartended for "singles clubs" group meetings. I felt sorry for these people. They had already ruined or destroyed someone's life and now they are looking to destroy someone else's. I again thought, "THERE MUST BE A BETTER WAY."

WHY WOMEN ARE REALLY OUT THERE

A friend could introduce you to someone he knows or you might meet someone at work. That is very good. However, if you want a bigger number of choices in your life, you have got to get out there with the knowledge of how to pick up a beautiful woman. Just do it!

Women want to feel special. They are looking for a little excitement in their lives, but not the way we are. Women are not looking for immediate excitement. To us, meeting a beautiful woman in a bar and having sex with her ten minutes later out in the car is a perfect evening. Wait, that's not a perfect evening. I forgot, it's not a perfect evening until you come back in and laugh about it with your friends. Now that is a perfect evening. What could be better? Believe me I understand, but they don't.

The kind of excitement they are looking for is a little bit more long term. You are just going to have to be a little patient.

ONE FROM THE HEART

A woman thinks from the heart. She thinks and feels at the same time. She thinks emotionally. I know that is hard to understand, but it is essential that you understand the way a woman thinks. This understanding is power in your hands.

If a woman feels in her heart that you are Mister Wonderful, there would be no way of dissuading her. You could have an encyclopedia full of evidence proving how bad you were. It would not matter.

No matter what reason a woman has for going out that night, there is an underlying, illuminating reason why she is there. She may be by herself and thinking she was just sick of looking at the four walls, or she just wanted to get out for a night. The real underlying reason is that she hopes to meet a nice guy who will bring some excitement into her life.

One girl might ask her girlfriend, "Do you want to go out for a drink and talk for a while?" Again, the underlying reason is the hope that they might meet some nice guys who will bring some excitement into their lives. Even if three or four girls go out together and sit in a booth, seemingly locked away from the rest of the club, they too are looking for the same possibility. Later on in the book, I will tell you the secrets of how to approach the female who is alone. Also, how to approach two females who are together and the secrets of how to approach a table full of girls, and successfully get the one you had your eye on.

BAD GIRLS

There is a small percent of women in lounges that are willing to have sex with you the same night. I would not advise doing that now-a-days, but I know a lot of you who don't seem to worry about it. My biggest concern is AIDS. Today's AIDS problem is something so serious, that I really don't want to get into it in this book. My word to the wise is BE CAREFUL.

So, why do so many guys use these girls all the time? I have known many of these girls for years. They have no problem meeting a guy, having a few drinks, and then going with him and having sex. To the guy, it feels like a conquest. He never saw the girl before. He doesn't know how many men she has been with. But to him, he thinks he's special. He thinks he is really doing something great. He thinks he went out, picked up a girl, and, because he is so irresistible, she had sex with him. He has a feeling of accomplishment. He thinks the challenge was met, and that he was in control. "Mucho macho." But believe me, it was not "mucho macho," it was probably "mucho stupid" for having sex with such a promiscuous woman.

I have been trying for over twenty years to warn you guys on the spot about these kinds of women. We refer to them in the business as "bimbos." I would say, "be careful, this girl has been around, if you know what I mean." But it does not seem to matter. Once you guys zero in on something, it seems nothing I could say will change your mind. If you find a woman giving up sex to you easily, she probably did the same thing to the last hundred, maybe thousand, guys.

So don't think you're something special. Practice safe sex, for God's sake, if you must go with these kinds of women. About those huge bimbos, stay as far away as possible from those extra crispy, big bucket ones.

When you are finished reading this book, you will not have to go after that kind of woman. You will be able to get the most beautiful woman you want and have more choices than you ever imagined.

This book will enable you to have the bold, fearless belief in yourself, to walk up to any beautiful woman you want and have her for your own. After you learn the secrets, and just try them out once, you will know the true power of this knowledge. You will have confidence in your own abilities.

MEN MAKE THINGS HAPPEN

Let us go back 100,000 years for a minute. The female would sit in the cave waiting for us to bring home the food. She would wait for us to carry the firewood that would keep them warm. The female would watch us move the boulders out of the way to make a clear path in front of the cave. The female always waited for us to make things happen. A lot of that is true today. The female will get dressed up, put on her make-up, and go out to the club. She expects you to know what you are doing when it comes to relating to her in the proper way.

The female was brought up to be the non-aggressor. Just look at some TV programs women have been watching.

Let us start with "Donna Reed." Donna was the little homemaker who took care of the family, and never worked outside the home. "Father Knows Best" infers that the woman take the non-aggressive role. "Leave it to Beaver," again, the female is non-aggressive. "I Love Lucy." Lucy always tried to please Dezi. "The Dick Van Dyke Show." Laura was always the non-aggressor. The list goes on and on. Even in "The Addams Family," Morticia waited for Gomez to initiate the romance by kissing her hand all the way up to her shoulder.

Even today, the woman who is supposed to be more independent and self-sufficient is still brainwashed about her submissive roll when it comes to initiating romance.

Most women feel out of place when initiating a meeting for romantic purposes. They feel awkward, and they think it is improper for them to approach a male. These feelings are derived from the many TV programs and their own personal upbringing. Their own mothers taught them that this is an "unlady like" behavior. They are taught that a woman should be demure and reserved in her behavior. Anything else is considered "fast" or "cheap."

WHAT WOMEN EXPECT FROM YOU

This beautiful woman of your dreams is sitting there expecting you to be an individual who is open emotionally. Someone who is understanding, willing, and able to express his feelings.

She also expects you to understand her feelings. This might sound impossible to you as a man, but, as impossible as it may seem, these are qualities you will have to portray to have this beautiful woman. Remember, women are very intuitive. It is something inherent to them.

So, you'll have to develop these qualities some way. You don't have to be a pro at this. If you just appear to have these qualities, you're 99% there. If they feel you are trying, they will be more than willing to give you a chance.

This beautiful woman you are going to approach, is interested in what sort of potential you may have. She is thinking into the future. She is thinking what sort of potential your job may have. She thinks in the long term, not in the immediate, the way men do.

Basically, a woman knows nothing about being romantic. She has some ideas about how she would like to be romanced, but she does not do the romancing. That is your job. She knows that someday she will be cooking and cleaning and taking care of the family, but that's not very romantic. A romantic type of guy is very appealing throughout the relationship.

WOMEN NEED RELATIONSHIPS

Let us look at this beautiful woman sitting at the bar who looks so perfect and proper. She looks so unapproachable. In reality, she is so desperate for love. She is desperate for a relationship with someone. She would give up her family and friends, almost anything, to have a relationship with you. She might tell you she belongs to a dance club or a theatre group. She might tell you how many friends she has or how busy she is with her social calendar. But she would give up all these things just to have a relationship with a man.

What is underneath that beautiful facade is a million emotional crutches and wheelchairs, all reaching out to you. What seems inaccessible, unattainable, or unreachable is there for you once you have learned the secrets of beautiful women.

WOMEN FEEL INFERIOR

You are thinking you're not good enough to approach such a beautiful woman. But all the while she already feels inferior. Just talking to a beautiful woman for a few minutes, if you listen, will reveal this. She will tell you how she is no good at this or has no talent when it comes to that. Or perhaps her job is not that great and so on. She is constantly putting herself down during the conversation.

You know women are complicated. Just their private area alone requires a special doctor. That's right, a whole guy just for that area. They should have a whole building just for that area. No, they should have a theme park just for that area. I know I'd visit it.

MEN SHOULD KNOW EVERYTHING

You know, as men, we are expected to know about everything in this world. But, some things are impossible to know. You can pick up a book on algebra, science, history, or language, but there are just no books to read, until now, about how to get that beautiful girl you want.

It is not your fault, believe me. There was just no way of knowing how to do it. In the past, you had to go out and make a fool of yourself or just not try at all. Most guys would pick the latter because that was the safest way.

There are books about the problems of relationships, but no book about how to start a relationship. We read these books about saving our existing relationships because, as a people, we don't have that many choices. So we take what we get and try to make the best of it, but it just does not work.

After reading this book, you will have as many choices as you want. We all know that when we meet someone who is just not right for us, most of the time we stick with them because there are just no other choices.

With this book, you will have one beautiful woman after another. If one does not feel right, you just get another until you find the one that has all the right qualities you want.

If I didn't interview thousands of women over the past twenty-three years, I would not have known the secrets locked in their beautiful heads. But now the barriers are down, the mysteries are solved, and they are all yours.

A SENSITIVE STORY WOMEN LOVE

This actually happened to me in my life and it turned out to be the best way to get a woman interested in me as a person. Each time the subject of pets came up during a conversation with a woman, I would tell this story and would become irresistible to her. The story incorporates a kitten that was hit by a car on the street where I was traveling. I would tell the woman about this incident where I stopped my car and picked up the injured kitten, brought it home and nursed it back to health. I would go into detail about how I had to use an eye dropper to feed the kitten for a few weeks until it was able to stand and eat on its own. The kitten and I became very fond of each other, and it is my household pet to this day. This story hits women in the heart because they feel that I am a sensitive and humane individual. Women usually express a great preference toward men who have a wide array of socially desirable personality traits. They gravitate towards men who can be stirred by emotion. They feel that if you can be that sensitive to a stray cat on the street, how much more sensitive can you be toward their feelings. I give you permission to use this story the next time the subject comes up. It would be even better if you had a story similar to this that actually did happen to you in your life. If that is impossible, simply use this one.

2

PERSUASION

YOU WANT THE BEAUTIFUL WOMAN TO LEAVE WITH YOU

The art of persuasion is a very powerful tool when you are out in the field. What is your objective? Your objective is to persuade this beautiful woman at the other side of the bar to leave with you and no one else. Above all, not to leave by herself. In her mind, this is the most likely way, she feels, she will be leaving. Most women usually feel that probably nothing will happen, and she will be leaving alone.

She would like to meet a nice guy and stop for coffee or exchange phone numbers, but she feels that it is unlikely. You have to persuade this beautiful woman to make that choice. You have to make her want to leave with you. You have to make her feel good about this decision.

This woman already wants to leave with a nice guy. Now, all you have to do is make her believe that you are that guy. You are halfway there already.

She has to feel that she is going to be a happier person for meeting you and leaving with you. It is not so hard to imagine yourself in her position. She needs a companion and a friend. She is lonely, vulnerable, and needs a little excitement in her life. It is your job to prove that you are the man to do it.

Never let her think that you are trying to pick her up, but that you are looking for a relationship with someone.

Look this lady in the eye to see what is going on behind those eyes. There once was a Chinese proverb about the size of the eye pupils. If the pupils get bigger than usual, that means they want whatever you are selling.

The eyes are a good indicator as to how you are doing. Occasionally look into the eyes of the one you are trying to persuade. If you don't, she will think you are not truthful and, therefore, not trustworthy.

Make it easy and safe for her to leave with you. If you want her to have coffee with you after you are finished with the nightclub, have her drive her car to a well lit diner. You will follow in your car. Do not ask her to come in your car to the diner with you. Especially after a first chance meeting. In these times, a woman is very afraid (paranoid) to go with a man they really do not know that well.

She will only agree to this after you have convinced her that you are a nice guy, worthy of her interest.

All along you should be persuading her to make choices she feels good about. Make sure there are no penalties involved in these choices. For example:

- Fear of being alone with you where there are no other people.

- The inconvenience of driving alone to a far off diner.

- Not getting enough sleep for the next day, especially if she has work in the morning.
- Having to pay for coffee or breakfast at the diner.
- Trying to get too close to her, whereas making her feel uncomfortable.

Keep all your persuasion in an arena that she will feel very comfortable with. Make it easy for her to say yes. If she says no to something, try to turn it around by figuring out what the problem is and eliminating the "penalty" involved for her. This might make it possible for her to go with you.

LACK OF PERSUASION

I have seen this happen many, many times. A guy walks up to a woman and asks her to dance. She refuses and he just walks away, taking it for rejection. If I had a nickel for every time this has happened, I could fill a bra big enough to dwarf the great pyramids.

Ninety percent of the time this is not a rejection. She just does not feel like dancing. It is as simple as that. So the guy thinks he has been rejected, goes back to his bottle of Budweiser, and sucks on that the rest of the night. Walking up to a beautiful woman and asking her to dance is a bad approach, yet ninety-nine percent of you guys use it. You will understand how to approach a woman later on in this book. We will also discuss rejection in depth later. However, after you read this book, you should not be facing rejection.

Do you think for one minute that this woman sitting across the bar from you is happy to be alone for the night? Of the thousands of women I have interviewed over the past twenty-three years, not one of them was happy being alone. Taking a shower, getting dressed, putting on make-up and driving to the club alone is a sorry way to spend an evening. Even if two girls go out together (or three or four), they are not really happy. They would drop their best friend to go out with a nice guy in a minute. So when you see two or three or even four girls all looking like they are having a good time, they are not. They all are thinking they could be having a much better time if they were with someone of the opposite sex.

YOU ARE THE MAN SHE HAS WAITED FOR

Okay, now we know what is important to them. Now your power of persuasion must make them realize that you are the guy they have been looking for their whole lives. By going with you, they get the rewards they have been dreaming about.

You are persuading her even before you walk up to her, whether you know it or not. From the minute she saw you, the persuasion process starts the gears moving. This is one of the most crucial points in persuasion. I'll get into what to say to help break the ice - so to speak - later on in this book, but for now you must persuade her into feeling positive about you while you are in her sight.

When you are approaching her, she is thinking, "Is talking to this guy going to make me feel good or bad? Does he look nice, clean, and friendly? I'd like to talk to someone, but I don't want to be imposed upon. I hope this is not just another jerk. Should I talk or not? Is this going to be good for me or bad?"

You can dispel most of these fears by just smiling and approaching in a gentle, friendly manner. Much of the technique of persuading people is giving them rewards. While you are talking to this beautiful girl, spend a few dollars. Buy her a drink. She will feel good about that. You see, she feels she is getting something out of talking to you. She is starting to feel positive already. But, don't buy it ahead of time. Wait until she is finished with her drink and needs another. When you try to buy a woman a drink before she is ready, you are telling her something she does not appreciate. Subliminally you are saying, "Hurry up and drink so I can get you drunk and take advantage of you." Or, "You are probably going to need a lot to drink to talk to me." Or, "The only way I know how to make a woman happy is by using my money." Just wait until her glass is empty, and it looks like she may want another. Then offer to buy her a drink.

It helps to persuade this beautiful woman into thinking that you are like an old friend. After you find out what her name is, ask what her friends call her. Maybe it is a nickname or a short form of her real name. Then call her by that name. She will start feeling more comfortable with you.

Find out what church or synagogue she belongs to and try to relate it to yours. See what values she has and try to relate them with your values (if you have any, that is). Just kidding, a lot of guys I know don't have values. They just want sex with a beautiful woman. And I can understand, believe me I do. But getting back to the original idea. By relating with her on these points, you become like someone she has known all her life. She becomes very comfortable with you. You are persuading her to feel good about you. You are gaining a lot of leverage.

Do not jump ahead of yourself. Make sure she enjoys talking with you, having a drink with you, and even dancing with you. (Knowing how to dance is very important.) Before you ask her to go for coffee or breakfast, make sure you have persuaded her up to that point on all these things we covered. Once she feels you are an okay guy to talk to, have a drink with, and to dance with, it stands to reason that you are the right guy to leave with. Right? Well maybe. She still may not want to leave with you. Don't take this as a rejection. That may not be the way she plays ball. She may have something else in mind. Be open to that. She may just want to exchange phone numbers at this time. Don't be a fool, take the number and be happy. Remember, you have nothing but time. The next time you call her, she will be all yours. Besides, if you follow this book, you will have more phone numbers of beautiful women at your disposal than you ever imagined.

If you get a flat no on going out for coffee or getting the phone number, look back on what you might have done wrong during the persuasion process. Go all the way back to the beginning, to see if you made any mistakes with her and correct them. Maybe it was something you said about women in general that she did not like. Or something you said happened between your last girlfriend and you. But find out what you said wrong and correct it. Reinforce the things you talked about that made her seem happy.

It is like helping someone to dive off a high diving board. First you take them up a few feet and you let them dive at that level. Then a few more feet until finally, it is easy for them to take the high dive because you have gradually brought them up to that point.

Keep it as simple as possible. Don't make the evening seem complicated or ask her to do anything too confusing. If she seems to agree to stop for a cup of coffee with you, keep it as simple as that. Don't try to change the plans and go someplace that is hard for her to remember the directions to. Or a place that is too far from her home. Do not give her anything else to consider, or think about, that might bring up questions in her mind.

Bring up a doubt in her mind if you feel that your persuasion is not strong enough. Ask her if she is sure that she wants to pass up the possibility of having a nice relationship. Of going out together for dinner in nice restaurants. Possibly attending the theatre or plays with you. Lead her to think she may be losing something if she says no. Having a nice relationship with someone is exactly what she wants. So let her feel that she might lose that if she says no to you.

BE CONFIDENT, CONVINCING, AND TRUTHFUL

Be self-confident with a woman. By the way, after you use these techniques, and you see just how easy it is to get what you want, there will be an aura of self-confidence about you.

Be convincing with your persuasion. Plant nice suggestions into the minds of those beautiful women you want. Remember, you are a display window trying to conjure up curiosity for her to look further inside.

Be truthful during your persuasion. One of the biggest complaints I hear from beautiful women is that they are sick of all the "bullshit" we have been throwing around.

They know when they are being "bullshitted." So what is the use of doing it. They are not impressed. It makes them feel that we think they are stupid enough to believe this stuff. Stick to the truth, you can't go wrong. Everybody is not rich or the president of IBM. Besides, that is not what they are looking for anyway.

They are looking for a guy who is truthful - not selfish, means what he says, is courteous, and somebody with a set of values.

Try to keep her unaware of any alternatives there may be. Don't let her think there might be other possibilities tonight, other than you. Lead her to believe that it is perfectly natural for the both of you to get together.

BE ADVENTUROUS

During your persuasion process, tell her how nice it is to do something a little adventurous for a change. Do not make it too adventurous, just a little. A little exciting, just to get out of that rut. Notice I used the word "little." If she thinks it is too exciting or too adventurous, you can forget it. Do not ask her to go sky diving or pulling any rip cords the first time you meet her. To a woman, dancing with you or stopping for a cup of coffee can be exciting enough. Don't expect much more for the first meeting.

Do not talk about your problem with drinking or your problem with drugs. Don't mention the problem with your last girlfriend or even the problems you are having with your mother. Steer as far away from your problems as possible. Let her talk about her problems.

BROADEN YOUR CHOICES

Whether you can believe it or not, most beautiful women have more problems than most regular people. So listen to her problems and be sympathetic. People love sympathy, they eat it up.

Make her believe that this is a chance in a lifetime you both shouldn't pass up. Tell her that you think this could be a relationship you both should not let go by. Ask her to take a chance, just to find out. She will never forgive herself if she does not try, thinking what might have been. Tell her that sometimes you just have to make decisions for yourself. Tell her a relationship is something she is looking for anyway, and you are the one to give it to her.

You see, once you grasp the power of this book, you will understand that people, especially beautiful women, do not have many choices in their lives. So, they are bound to be persuaded to go with you. There are very few choices in her life to begin with, so how could she say no to a man who has the understanding this book will give him. You'll be the one with all the choices.

Play up the down side of your persuasion a little. Explain to her that there really are not many choices, or opportunities, for meeting nice people that you can have a relationship with. Nobody wants to be reminded of the downside, but subtle reminders will reinforce what you want. And that is to have that beautiful woman eventually. She knows her choices are limited, so a little reinforcement will help her decide that she should try you out. Besides, what can she lose.

A lot of times you will find beautiful women recovering from a broken relationship. We will elaborate on this later in the chapter on "Secrets of Beautiful

Women." During your persuasion process, find out what it was that caused the relationship to break up and try to relate with her on that point. If it was because he treated her badly, make sure you sympathize with her. Explain to her how well your father treated your mother, and that you feel no one should be treated badly, no matter what the circumstances. No matter what the situation was in their previous relationship, make sure you take her side. Besides, ninety-nine percent of the beautiful women I have interviewed over the past twenty-three years were jerked around by their former boyfriends. We can't help it, that's just the way we are. But please, don't ever admit it, or tell anybody I said so.

If you follow these tactics that I have outlined for you, you won't have any trouble getting beautiful women. The only way you might fail is if she won't pay ANY attention to you at all or she's deaf or doesn't speak English. But, if you use one of the opening lines given to you in this book, which creates the stimulus, and you get her attention, there is no way you can possibly fail. Remember, now you have her attention, and you are selling her something she already wants. It is not like she does not want this to begin with.

SHAKE IT

You have made your approach and used your opening line, now offer to shake her hand. Men shake hands all the time with each other. When we shake hands with another man, we are implying that we are equal. This is an equal start. Women want to know today that they are equal. They want an equal start too. Most of the time when we meet a man and a woman, we shake hands with the man, acknowledging he is an equal. Then, when we are introduced to the woman, we usually don't shake her hand, acknowledging that she is not equal. Therefore, not starting on the same level.

Are you beginning to see how much persuading you are doing just by following these simple rules?

With the simple handshake, she feels you are recognizing her power and respecting her as a person. This puts her in an open and receptive position to you. Now, with what you have learned from this book, you cannot lose.

Think of it like this, how much persuasion goes on around a person in a days time. Between the radio and television, hundreds of products are trying to get people to purchase them. All of them trying to persuade people to do something. On the other hand, how many people are trying to persuade this beautiful woman to be with them? Not very many, I'm afraid. Perhaps a friend of hers knows a guy or maybe someone at work jokingly hits on her from time to time. But really, no one actually tries to persuade her to be with them, because they simply don't know how.

WOMEN'S FEARS

Women have other fears that work in our favor. Usually their friends and family put pressure on them to find a nice guy. They add stress by telling her that she is "not getting any younger." You see, when a man and a woman are at a certain age, the woman is considered "over the hill," while the man is considered "in his prime." That is a double standard, but is does exist. I'm not saying it is right, just that it does exist for a woman.

TRY ME, I'M FREE

I'm sure you are aware of those free trial products that we all try because they are free with no obligation. That is a good policy for selling yourself to this beautiful woman you are talking to. Nothing heavy, just a free trial date (on you, or course) with no responsibility to her what-so-ever. A beautiful woman will be more inclined to go with you under these circumstances. Especially if she is rebounding from a heavy relationship that just went sour. It takes the pressure off of this beautiful woman and she feels she deserves a nice time without any strings attached.

EVE DID IT

Persuasion is a good thing. It has been here since Eve persuaded Adam to eat that damned apple. It goes on in everyone's life, every day of the year. But not many are the master of it. Just think of all the persuasion that has gone on in your life, and you probably don't even realize it. I don't have time to go into it now, but think of all the persuasion your mother and father alone have used to influence you. Why not be a master of it. Especially when it comes to getting something you really want. A pocket full of phone numbers of beautiful women at your disposal. Dozens of beautiful women at your beckon call. You can convince these beautiful women that you are the guy to go with. Why stand by and watch what you want get away when you can manipulate the situation to your advantage.

You are fulfilling a special need in your life and in hers. Although she might not know it yet, you are going to be the next man in her life. Your power of persuasion puts you in the drivers seat. You know what you want and, after reading this book, you'll know how to get it.

SCHOOL GIRLS

Everybody knows only one method. It stems back to when we were all in middle school or high school at the sock hop or weekend dance - whatever you want to call it. The boys were on one side and the girls were on the other. Now the boy has to initiate this boy-girl meeting. He would try to get up enough courage to go over and ask some girl he had his eye on to dance. If she says, "no, I don't feel like dancing right now," the boy has to walk all the way back across the dance floor (which feels like an eternity) to face a bunch of laughing peers. The boy is devastated. He feels like Count Dracula at the end of the movie, after someone drove a stake through his heart. We have not developed since that time we were boys in school.

We still do the same exact thing as adults, because that is all we know. Nobody had developed us in this area. Masters and Johnson taught us what happens when a male and a female are having sex. Their pulse, their breathing, what their sweat glands are doing. There are many books about relationships and why they break up. But there is no way to develop from that boy walking across the dance floor, to the man walking through the nightclub. There was no way to become a man with an educated, developed mind, knowing what he wants and how to get it.

PERSISTENCE

Remember when you were a little boy and you wanted something, but your mother said no? You would not take no for an answer. You kept being persistent. You knew that "no" didn't really mean "no." It meant "maybe." You never worried about rejection. You never got embarrassed. You just kept persisting and persisting until you got what you wanted. You might have been sent to your room for a while. You might have been told to sit on the couch quietly for a while. But eventually you got what you wanted in the end. Well, basically, the same theory applies here. Those same principles apply now just as they did years ago, when you wanted to get something from your own mother. You have to communicate with this beautiful woman and persuade her in a diplomatic and civil way. You must do this on a personal, one-on-one level and be persistent at the same time. Forget about being rejected. Forget about being embarrassed. Just keep persisting. (NOTE: This does not pertain to sex. If a woman says no, she means no.)

You have to remember that the beautiful woman you want must know that she is going to get something out of all this. Even your mom got something out of giving you what you wanted. Remember how you were such a good boy after you got what you wanted (for a little while anyway). The same thing applies here. You have to persuade this beautiful woman that she will gain "lots" by going out with you, but not monetarily.

MONEY, FRIENDSHIP, AND SAFETY

Beautiful women are not interested in your money. You have to convince her that she will gain friendship. Believe it or not, friendship is more important than money.

Companionship is another quality beautiful women are looking for. She also wants a suitable partner whom she feels safe with. I have to emphasize "safe," especially these days. It is so important to a woman to feel safe. The "today woman" is facing a very scary world. A place where just walking out to her car has become a terrifying experience. One of the biggest advantages to you is whether you can project the image of someone who is safe and trustworthy.

Just the market for guns alone sold to women in this country lately, should tell you something about how insecure they feel today. By making it a win situation for her, you are making it a win situation for you too.

WHAT SHE EXPECTS

When a beautiful woman goes out for the night, she expects certain things to happen. She expects the music to be loud, the room to be smokey, and people to be there. She expects the bartender to ask her what she would like to drink. All these things she has decided ahead of time. There is no real decision making going on in her head about any of these things, except you. You are the one that is going to set the decision process going. Now she has to start making decisions and choices that she really did not expect to make. You now have to know what to do and say in order to get the decision making process going in your favor.

DECISIONS, DECISIONS, DECISIONS

Don't waste time when you see that beautiful woman. Make your move. This prevents anyone else from approaching her, and it also sends a message into her mind that there are probably no alternatives anyway. We are all brought up believing that opportunity only knocks once, so use that sort of brainwashing to your advantage. You are eliminating her problem of making all those decisions concerning other guys, because you are making yourself her only choice. She came out to enjoy herself, not to make a million decisions if she doesn't have to.

People in general do not like making too many decisions. We are creatures of habit. We, as guys, may have to do a little more work, but believe me, it is well worth it. Lead her to believe that what she would naturally do in this situation is the right thing to do. That for the time being, she is better off talking to you than doing anything else.

She has some idea in her mind about what kind of man she would like to talk to. And it is very simple, believe me, I know. I have interviewed thousands of beautiful women. You must read the chapter on "Interviews With Two Thousand Beautiful Women" to understand what I mean. If you follow the suggestions in Chapter 6, you will not cause her to have any anxiety in the first few minutes of your meeting. Any other behavior will cause her to start a real effort at decision making that both you and her do not want. Because, if you are not what she expects or prefers in those first few minutes, you might as well forget it.

Remember, she has an idea of what she wants from another human being. It's not like buying some clothes. She might not mind trying something different when it come to that. But when deciding on a man, she does not want to try something other than that which she has in mind. It is just too complicated and confusing. It's too big of a chance to take. So study the interviews later in this book and know what these beautiful women expect. Do not try to deviate from it for the time being.

WHAT'S HER TYPE

With the thousands of women I have interviewed over the years, I have noticed that a certain percent favor a particular type of man. It is to your advantage, during the course of your conversation, to find out what she liked about her previous boyfriends. Then incorporate that into the type of things you like to do. Stay in the flow of things that she has already decided on. Don't stray too much to the right or left. You have to ring that bell in her head that says, "everything is alright with him so far." That little bell tells her that you're all the things she expects and that eventually she will be leaving with you.

SUPPRESS THOSE HORMONES

Remember, women do not have that hormonal drive that we have. As a man in a nightclub, you have to take that drive and suppress it the best that you can. If she feels that the reason you are giving her your attention is for a sexual purpose, or she detects it in the slightest way, you are sunk. You're dead in the water.

BIMBOS

Her choosing to leave with you will be strictly based upon the reasons given in this chapter, and not for any sexual ones. If it is strictly sex that you want, there are plenty of women in the clubs who are out for that reason too, and this book will get you a hundred of them tonight if you want. As I mentioned earlier, in the "biz" we call them "bimbos." Just watch out for those big fat ones - you know, that "bimboasaurus." I wouldn't recommend getting anywhere near their gravitational pull if I were you. Give them a wide berth or you might just get sucked in, if you know what I mean. The women who are out and are willing to have sex with you the first time they meet you, usually have some kind of problem. They are doing it because that is the only way they can get the attention they crave. Or they might have some other problem. Either way, it is a bad bet now-a-days, especially with AIDS lurking out there.

Believe me, they are not afraid of AIDS. It does not scare them in the least. They will have sex with you and the next night have sex with another guy. It's just no problem to them. As I stated before, if you have to have sex with these women, use every precaution there is available to you to protect yourself.

As a male, I know that sex drive we all have. But, today, you have to use your head. This instructional book will enable you to get the best, most beautiful woman you could imagine. You won't have the need for that "bimbo" type of woman. You will have any number of women to choose from.

SUM IT UP

So let us try to sum up what we have been talking about in this chapter on persuasion. You walk into a club. You see this beautiful woman. She may be alone, with a girlfriend, or with a group of friends. With the skill and techniques outlined in this chapter, you will persuade her into leaving with you before the night has ended. You will need to know what is going on in her mind. You will then be able to fulfill what she has predetermined she wants in a man. You will already have a good idea of what she expects after reading this book, studying this chapter, and reading my interviews with beautiful women. You will, so to speak, ring all the right bells in her head concerning the way you approach her, your personality, the way you dress, how friendly you appear, and all the other qualities outlined. This will give her no choice but to decide that you have everything required to escort her on whatever adventure you two may encounter.

Stick to the outlined information and you can't go wrong. With the over twenty years I've put into nightclubs, and the thousands of interviews I have done, you now know what is going on in these beautiful heads. And you know how to make that work for you. What better advantage could a person have.

3

BODY LANGUAGE

Communicating with the body is as old as man himself. We have been doing it since the beginning of time. We all do it, yet most of us don't even realize we are doing it. As I said earlier, subtle gestures can be neon signs to those who know how to read them. It is important that you recognize these signs. They tell you when to approach, how you are doing, and when you are going too far. A beautiful woman can be communicating with you, and you might not even know it, if you don't understand body language. When deaf people communicate with each other through different hand and arm signals, we are completely baffled by it. But to them, it makes perfect sense. Exactly the same thing is happening between this beautiful woman and you. It is a big mistake to be baffled by it.

In this chapter, I will take you from the most extreme cases of body language to the most subtle. Let us cover the most extreme cases of body language which I have experienced in the past twenty-three years.

I have seen women expose their whole breast to men, by either slowly pulling down their sweater or opening their blouse to reveal a breast (or two). I have seen women sucking or licking their thumbs in a manner that would suggest fellatio. I have also seen women, with a slit up the middle of the skirt, cross and uncross their legs to reveal no panties underneath. You don't have to be a genius to figure out what these body language suggestions mean. All in all, it is still body language. It is communicating without speaking, isn't it? But there is a more sophisticated body language that goes on continuously.

This is especially true in the nightclubs where the mating ritual is so prevalent. It is the nightclub where seasoned body language is trumped-up to an art. You can be speeding down the highway at night, but without a radar detector beeping away, you would never know someone was out to get you. You have got to have the right equipment in the nightclub to detect what is coming your way.

THE EYES HAVE IT

If a lovely woman has an interest in a man, one of the first things to notice is the whites of her eyes. That's right, the whites of her eyes. If you are seeing more white than usual, she is very interested. Remember that old saying, "Don't shoot until you see the whites of their eyes"? Well, if it were a woman they were talking about, it would have read, "Don't start getting undressed until you see the whites of their eyes."

Not only the whites of her eyes, but also the pupils. If the pupils seem dilated, this means she is seeing something she wants real bad

If you make eye contact with a beautiful woman, and she doesn't intend it to mean anything, it will usually last only a second. She will then look away. But, if the eye contact lasts a fraction of a second longer, she is trying to convey an alluring message. Many emotions can pass through the body language of the eyes. A woman can portray that glazed look of love through her eyes. If her eyes drop to your pelvic area, she will be projecting a seductive gaze. When you don't see much white in her eyes, that is not a good sign - be leery of that. If you are not looking her in the eyes when you are talking to her, she will know you are full of "bull." Believe me, beautiful women are sick of being "bull shitted" by us. It is better to stick to the truth, no matter what it is.

When you see a beautiful woman blinking at you, this is a good sign. This is a come-on sign. She wants you to come over and converse. The batting of the eye lashes, more often than not, is a courting gesture.

Winking is a bold thing for a woman to do. You won't find many women who do it. But you might find that if you wink at her, and she winks back - well, it is pretty obvious what that means. I think winking at the opposite sex is kind of an old-fashioned thing that you do not see much of in today's society.

STIFFEN UP

If she starts sitting straight up and her muscles seem firm, she is telling you, with body language, that she is interested. Look to see if her skin tone has become a little redder. She is telling you she is excited by your presence, and continue to come a little closer. Even her face will seem a bit redder. Any gravitational pull on her facial muscles will stiffen up and she will even appear younger. Any movement of the thighs or pelvic region are dead giveaways of body language. These are seductive, sexual body movements designed to let you know that things could happen, if you want them to.

Watch for a constant stroking or playing with her hair when you are looking within her perimeter. If she's twirling it around her fingers while she is looking your way, these are signs of readiness. Any touching of her ears or earrings and sliding her hand behind her head to fluff up her hair, are sure signs that she wants you to approach her. If you see the palms of her hands facing you, this is a sign that she is ready to take whatever you are giving.

If you see a woman sitting with her breasts protruding straight out in your direction, she is all yours. (Don't run over and grab them, however.) Just know this is body language.

WATCH HOW SHE SITS

If a beautiful woman is sitting on a bar stool (or in a booth), and she is slowly stroking her thighs or her wrists, these are come-on signs of body language.

She might be sitting on a bar stool; facing the dance floor with her legs crossed. Her skirt high enough to reveal her thighs while resting one hand on her hip. These are also come-on signals.

You might see her running her finger nails along the top of her blouse, up and down to the top of her cleavage. Sometimes you will notice that the top button is open, revealing a lot of cleavage, implying that there is a possibility of you unbuttoning the rest of the blouse.

POINT IT OUT TO ME

Some of the more subtle body language is when she is leaning a bit in your direction. Or the foot of the leg that crosses over is pointing in your direction. Or any of her limbs are pointing in your direction. Even if three people are having a conversation and her legs are crossed with her foot pointing in your direction, this means you are the focus of her attention. This also applies when a woman's legs are crossed, and she is rocking that top leg back and forth in front of you.

If you should lean into her immediate area, and she leans toward you or is not disturbed by your apparent closeness, these are signs of acceptability to you. If she leans back or relocates to a different area, that is not a good sign for you. It does not necessarily mean a rejection. It just means that she is not ready for you to occupy her immediate space yet.

Her immediate space is the border around her that she claims as hers. The space that she feels comfortable with. It could cover one or two feet around herself that she does not want anyone to enter yet.

CRUSH THE COMPETITION

If you feel you are reading the body language correctly, and you approach, yet her eyes shift to another male in the area, this does not mean a rejection to you. Perhaps you are not the only male she is interested in at the moment. Don't let this bother you, because after reading this book, you will know just what to say and do to eliminate any competition.

SHE GIVES YOU THE BRUSH

What seems like an accidental touch, or if a woman brushes by you on her way to the rest room, is usually not an accident. Touching is one of the more direct body language approaches. A woman will very rarely resort to this approach unless she is getting absolutely nowhere with her subtle body language.

SMOKE SIGNALS

Remember when Tonto and the Lone Ranger used to read the smoke signals that the Indians sent up? Well, you will need to have a little "Lone Ranger" in you to read the smoke signals in the nightclub.

More women smoke now than ever before. As a matter of fact, it was sociably unacceptable for women to smoke in public for the longest time. But now, the cigarette has become a form of body language to get your attention.

In the dim atmosphere of a nightclub, the cigarette becomes a beacon, like a light house, drawing the male in. Every time a female draws in on the cigarette, it lights up brightly. And by doing so attracts attention to her, like lightning bugs at dusk. The cigarette becomes almost hypnotic. The female rests her elbow on her hip with the cigarette between her fingers, waving it back and forth, leaving a smoke trail of S's. Almost like the curves of a woman's body. This fanning technique is a smoke signal calling attention to her availability.

The female places the cigarette between her lips, drawing the smoke in, wetting the lips with her tongue, and then blowing the smoke out. This possesses a very phallic movement associated with sex.

When a woman is holding a cigarette in her hand that is unlit, and flicking it around with her thumb, that is like a worm on a hook. She then takes some time finding a match in her pocket book. This is an open invitation for you to make your move.

If she is blowing smoke from her bottom lip up, approach should be a little more cautious. But, if she is blowing smoke straight out from between her lips, and in your direction, these are positive signs.

GETTING YOURSELF OUT OF TROUBLE

You can lie and falsify statements with words, but you can't lie with body language. If a woman feels you're coming on too strong, you will notice a different message coming at you. If she begins to turn slightly away from you, this means she is starting to get turned off. Stop whatever it is you are talking about and go onto something more suitable for her to listen to. If you start losing eye contact with her, she is becoming disinterested. If you notice her folding her arms across her chest, this means she is starting to close off to you. Crossing her legs is alright, but if she double crosses them at the ankle, you are in trouble. When skin tone starts to appear less red and muscles begin to sag, this also spells trouble.

HIGH HEELS

Those high heels that women wear are not on their feet because they are so comfortable. As a matter of fact, they are downright painful. But, the high heel pushes their buttocks up and out, and forces the muscles of the thigh to contract, giving them a trimmer appearance. This is the female's body language telling you that she is in sexual readiness.

SIX FOOT BLOND

Loud clothing is another way for a female to project body language. I can remember this beautiful blond who used to come into the club I worked. She had to be at least six foot one with her high heels on. She never moved, only to sip her drink. Even when she ordered her drink, she just said, "White wine on the rocks." Never smiled, never moved her eyes, just a dead stare. She paid her three dollars and fifty cents, picked up her change, never left a tip, and never said anything else. The bar was usually three people deep, and she just stood there - one arm down by her side, sipping her drink with the other hand. No one ever approached her. They just stared at her. She just stared at the band and dancers.

I noticed that guys, during the course of the evening, would work their way over to her through the crowd and just stand next to her. Never even saying "boo" to her. She was absolutely beautiful from head to toe. So, "what's the deal" you're probably asking yourself about this blond. Well, that is what I decided to find out. In most clubs I have worked, I knew everybody in the place. They were actually my friends. I saw them more than I saw my own family. And I liked everyone, from the biggest wise mouth guy to the most beautiful woman. I especially made a point to find out what made these beautiful women tick.

That's why, after more than twenty years, almost seven nights a week, I have learned everything about the art of picking up beautiful women. This was accomplished through my power of observation, and outright asking them what it would take to have a beautiful woman like themselves. I had established many friendships with these beautiful women and gained their trust over the years. It also made for a better rapport when I interviewed these women. You will have a number of these surveys to evaluate for yourself later on in this book.

Anyway, after a few times of serving this beautiful blond her white wine on the rocks, I decided to find out what the deal was. So, the next time she ordered I said, "Listen, have you ever tried White Zinfandel instead of that White Chablis you have been drinking? Let me give you a free sample. I think you'll find it tastes better." She tried it and said, "Thanks, I like it better than what I have been drinking. From now on serve me the Zinfandel ." Then she said, "By the way, you're the first person who's talked to me since I've been coming in here."

I felt like saying, "Well, you stand there like a pillar of salt, what do you expect?" But then I realized she was using body language. I realized why she wore tight spandex body suits and high heels. She was screaming with body language, only no one knew what to do about it. Many guys asked me about her, still, no one would approach her. Finally, a buddy of mine asked me about her. I told him not to worry about the way she looks, she is really just a regular person underneath, looking for someone.

I practically had to pry him out of his chair to get him over to her, so I could introduce her to him. They have been going out ever since.

After you read the surveys and the part of the book that deals with secrets of beautiful women, and you learn to read body language, you too will realize that no matter how beautiful a woman is, she can be yours any time you want.

STROKE IT

When you find the body language flashing all green lights at you, and you decide to make your approach, choose any one of the "Top Ten Opening Pickup Lines" outlined in this book to break the ice. If you notice that while you are talking to her she is slowly stroking her cocktail glass up and down with her thumb and pointer finger, this is an indicator that everything is going very well as far as she is concerned. This is a very sexual, rhythmic message, done in a subtle way.

IT'S VERY TOUCHING

Touching is a part of body language that is somewhat controversial. I have seen guys try to touch too soon. I have seen guys try to touch too much. The wrong touching can put her off almost immediately. Touching on the arm is sort of okay, as long as it is toward the back of the arm. Touching on the leg is not okay. You are communicating too much sex, and believe me, you don't want to do that. We will discuss this later, after you read the chapter on "Interviews With Two Thousand Beautiful Women." Try to perfect that "everything's going to be alright" doctor's touch you get when you visit the doctor. Especially when you make that first encounter with her. That first hand shake should be reassuring, gentle, and slightly firm. She should get the "everything's going to be alright" feeling right after that first encounter.

Your best bet is not to do much touching at all, if possible. Whatever touching you do, make sure it is the back of the arm or the back of the shoulder. You might slightly rub up and down, always relating through your touch that "everything is going to be alright." Remember when you were a kid, and your mother rubbed the back of your shoulder when you needed some reassurance? Well, that's exactly the same message you want to give this beautiful woman whom you are trying to convince to leave with you.

During your conversation, the band might choose to play a slow song. If you invite her to dance and she accepts, you may take her by the hand out to the dance floor or lead her by the back of the arm. When dancing for the first time with her, take all your hormones and testosterone, and tie it around the bar stool. Don't bring it out on the dance floor with you. Don't start grabbing and squeezing at everything. If you reveal that your interest in her is strictly sexual, YOU'RE FINISHED! Strap on your hormones and testosterone and head for the door, because you're out of there.

The normal, occasional brushing of the skin, or the bodies brushing together, is alright. It can't be helped when you are dancing a slow dance with a woman. But, don't bring it to any other level than that.

THE UNSPOKEN LANGUAGE

Remember, there was a time when mankind did not have a language to communicate with each other. During the caveman era, there was no language. It was all body language. Yet, they managed to create the population of the world through body language alone. Body language was the earliest form of communication known to man. There was no way of telling anyone what you had on your mind. It all came out through body language, either consciously or subconsciously.

Since we had developed a spoken language, we felt no need for body language. We thought that since we can communicate so well with a spoken language, why bother with studying body language. There is more truth and feeling in body language than any spoken communication.

SMILE A LITTLE SMILE FOR ME

When a woman smiles at you, and you see both her upper and lower teeth, and the muscles in the face that cause the smile are not tense, this is a good sign for you. However, if you see both sets of teeth and the muscles in the face seem tense and the smile does not brighten up the face, this is simply a polite smile with no connotation what-so-ever. If she smiles with both lips tightly drawn in, she is feeling a bit depressed, or even inferior, to you.

PICK YOUR POCKET

When you see a woman opening her pocketbook more often than usual, this is an open invitation, or green light, to you. She is trying to tell you that she is open for you to come in. If her thumb is inside the pocketbook, just lingering there, this is a courting gesture to you.

TOUCHING THE FACE

Any touching of the nose is usually not a good sign for you. It usually means "no good," "forget it," "you're not for me."

When you see a woman with her fingernail between her teeth, this means that she is contemplating the idea of you and her relating in some way. This also applies to touching the cheek or rubbing the chin.

HEAD MOVEMENT

When a woman tosses her head back and moves her head from side to side, causing her hair to move back and forth suddenly, she is looking to get your attention for some kind of encounter.

If a woman cocks her head when she becomes aware of your presence, this means she is quite interested in finding out more about you.

If a woman is showing her wrists to you in some way, possibly smoking with arm bent up and palm and wrist facing you, this also is a courting gesture. If she is rubbing her wrists slightly up and down, or stroking them, she's courting you.

Should a woman be looking at you over her shoulder with eyelids slightly lowered, and each time you look at her she drops her gaze, she is interested.

LIP SERVICE

Some women try to mimic their genital area with their mouth. If they keep their mouth slightly open and wet their lips by licking them, they are trying to portray the same look the genital area gets when she's hot and excited. Some women will wear lipstick with a lip gloss over it, to give that wet look of sexual excitement. The lips themselves will become poutier because of the blood flow that increases when a woman is stimulated by the way a particular man looks. Her nipples may start to protrude a little, and they will become more prevalent when she becomes excited over a man she admires.

A LEG UP

If a woman is wearing jeans, and her legs are open a little more than usual, with her genital area in your direction, this is her way of signaling that she may be available, under the right circumstances.

Crossing one leg over the other slowly and then back again while rubbing the thighs, is a positive sign.

You may see a woman sitting in a booth, kicking her shoe off and then putting her foot back in it. Or she may be sitting on a bar stool, dangling her shoe from her toes and slipping it on and off. This is that "in and out" motion associated with sexual intercourse and is a very positive signal to you.

Sometimes you notice a woman sitting on one leg with her other leg over it. Her thighs might be slightly open while she is wearing a dress. That is a come-on to you.

She may be sitting on the edge of the bar stool with one leg straight to the floor, while the other leg is crossed, but kept very high, so you can see that the muscles are flexed. This is a green light.

TWO BEAUTIES IN A BOOTH

Let me tell you a story about body language that involved two beautiful women.

Sometimes telling the events that I have seen personally may help you understand the nightclub scene better. I have seen so many things over the past twenty or so years, that I couldn't possibly put them all into one book. If I did, you would need a spotter to help you carry the book home.

This story involves body language and how to approach two or more women who are sitting in a booth, away from the action of the bar.

I noticed two beautiful women sitting in a booth, thirty feet from the band. One was a slightly framed blond with long, straight hair, that flowed all the way down her back and past her buttocks. She was about five feet six inches tall. The other was a brunette with long curly hair, perfectly proportioned with a beautiful face.

Each week they would come in, sit in the same booth, and order the same drinks. It looked like, to the unprofessional eye, that they were having a great time together. They would talk and laugh, have a few drinks, and dance with each other. But, I knew from their body language that there was much more to it than that.

Although they were relating to each other very well, their body language was saying something else. I noticed that one was kicking off her shoe and putting it back on again. Sharp glances over their shoulders at the action of the bar. Slowly crossing the legs, stroking the thighs, and licking the lips occasionally. All the telltale signs of body language that a trained eye can spot a mile away. So, I decided that the next time I took a break, I would stop at their table and find out what the story was with these two.

I waited until the band took a break so it wouldn't be too noisy, and then I approached their table. I used a variation of one of the "TOP TEN APPROACHES GUARANTEED TO WORK," discussed in this book later on. I said, "I couldn't help noticing that you two beautiful girls have been coming in here for weeks now, and you always sit at this table, away from the bar. There is no way for me to get to know either of you when you are so far away." They said, "We like to sit in the booth because it is always so crowded at the bar." I knew this wasn't true just from their body language alone. I'm not saying the girls were lying, I'm just saying that they probably felt more comfortable in the booth. But, they would have enjoyed themselves more, socializing at the bar and making new friends, especially with me.

So, I made that known to them. I told them that if I could possibly get at least one bar stool open for a start, would they come over and sit at the bar. They agreed that if I could, they would come over and stay in the area that I served drinks.

Now, do you see what has happened here with these two beautiful girls so far? I took a situation with two complete strangers, who happen to be beautiful, and made it work to my advantage. When I noticed their body language saying, "I want attention," I knew what to do. No matter what they told me with words about how they liked to sit in a booth, away from the crowds, I knew their body language could not lie.

Most guys who don't know better, and don't know the techniques in this book, would have walked away feeling rejected. That is, if they would have approached the table in the first place. Most guys would not dare to approach a table of beautiful girls to begin with.

When I approached the table, and I used a variation of one of the opening pickup lines outlined in this book, I incorporated the two girls and called both of them beautiful. I did not exclude either one. You'll find out why later on in this book.

I told the girls I would signal them the minute a stool was available. I instructed them to grab their drinks and run over before someone else takes it. I knew it would not be hard to get a stool available, because all I had to do is tell some guy at the bar, "Do you see those two beautiful girls over there in the booth? Well, if you get up, I'll bring them over here and maybe I'll even introduce you to them." So, you know damn well he was going to get up.

So, I signaled to them that I had a stool available. They came over, and we became good friends after that. Both of these girls were available to me from that time on. But, I never had time to take either one of them out. Remember, I was working almost every night, and I just didn't have time for every girl I met. Plus, I would set up arrangements like this almost every night. There was no way I could have possibly taken all these beautiful women out, even in ten lifetimes.

Anyway, getting back to the original story, here were two beautiful girls that anyone, who reads this book, could have had. I also hope you noticed how the techniques kept me in control of the situation at all times.

The girl I mentioned with the long blond hair used to stand most of the time, watching the dancers. And some guy, who never talked to her, used to pet her hair that flowed passed her buttocks. He thought no one noticed because it was so crowded. When she told me of this, I really did not know what to say. All I could think of was, if this man knew what to do and say to her, he would not have to stand behind her, touching her hair. He would have what he wanted.

The blond eventually moved to a different state. The brunette met a guy who was mean to her and hit her occasionally when he drank too much.

I thought, here was a beautiful girl who was

available for the longest time. She finally starts dating a guy, and he's mean to her. All the other guys who just looked at her at the bar, when she was available, could have had a good thing. But, they passed it up because she looked too beautiful to approach. Had they known the techniques in this book, they could have had her and many more.

A TONGUE LASHING

Getting back to other forms of body language. We talked about a woman licking her lips to make them appear wet and sexy. Well, any biting of the lips is a sexual courting technique. If a woman shows her tongue in any form, such as touching her front teeth with her tongue (especially when you can see the underside of the tongue) these are strong courting gestures. Tongues are very strong sexual devices used by women to show special interest.

JIGGLING THE JEWELRY

A woman might be playing with her jewelry. She could be stroking her necklace or pulling on it. She may be stroking or fiddling with her bracelet, especially if it is shiny or sparkles, and it catches your eye. This is almost like a "morse code" signaling a message to you. This is that sexual, stroking message, associated with sexual intercourse, that she is trying to send to you in a subliminal way, through body language.

SHE HAS A CERTAIN FLARE

Did you ever see a bull's nostrils flare when they get excited? Especially when Bugs Bunny flashes that red cape in front of the bull's face. His nostrils begin to flare and smoke comes out. Well, something a little more subtle happens when a woman gets excited at the sight of a man. You'll notice her nostrils begin to flare slightly at times.

FACE TO FACE

Men are taught from the beginning, as small boys, not to show emotion. Not to cry, not to show fear, so we have a little more control over our facial expressions than women do.

Women are taught to show all their emotions through the facial expressions. That's why it is much easier to figure out what a woman is thinking through her facial body language. From a lifetime of showing their emotions, they have no recourse but to express them. They can't help it, and it is our job to learn to read it to our advantage.

If you find a woman mirroring your body language, whether it be eye contact or any other body language sign outlined in this chapter, this means she is trying to make contact with you.

FEMALES HAVE PERFECTED BODY LANGUAGE

Since women have traditionally been the less aggressive of the two sexes, it stands to reason that they would have to communicate to the male through body language. Especially in the nightclub scene, where the female has perfected it to an art. The fact is that she cannot approach a male in a sociably accepted way (without being thought of as a hooker or a loose woman). And then there is the time factor. There is usually only a few hours between the time the band starts and "last call," for individuals to meet.

So, body language is an important factor in a female's life. If you put a female alone in a room, none of these body language techniques, outlined in this chapter, would be taking place. But, in an atmosphere where male and female mingle for a short period of time, and competition is fierce, body language becomes like neon signs flashing all around you.

Scientists who study body language call themselves Kinesic researchers. They would agree with mostly everything I have outlined in this chapter. However, I have never seen a scientist spend more than twenty years, almost seven nights a week, observing body language in nightclubs. So, we have gone beyond what they profess to know about body language.

Body language is a big factor for you to understand in your quest for that beautiful woman. But, body language alone is not enough. The full content of this book will get you what you want, guaranteed.

Don't just read the chapter on "Top Ten Opening Pickup Lines Guaranteed To Work" and go off with just that information. Yes, it will work to break the ice and start you off on the right foot, but it really helps to know what they want from that point on, to really land the deal.

STUDIES

Psychiatry 1978 Nov;41(4):346-59

The nonverbal basis of attraction: flirtation, courtship, and seduction.

Givens DB

According to a familiar phrase, the "language" of love is universal. Recent ethological studies of nonlinguistic communication in courtship using facial expression, gesture, posture, distance, paralanguage, and gaze have begun to establish that a universal, culture-free, nonverbal sign system may exist (Eibl-Eibesfeldt, 1975), which is available to all persons for negotiating sexual relationships. The nonverbal mode, more powerful than the verbal for expressing such fundamental contingencies in social relationships as liking, disliking, superiority, timidity, fear and so on, appears to be rooted firmly in man's zoological heritage (Bateson, 1966, 1968). Paralleling a vertebrate-wide plan, human courtship expressivity often relies on nonverbal signs of submissiveness (meekness, harmlessness) and affiliation (willingness to form a social bond). Adoption of a submissive-affiliative social pose enables a person to convey an engaging, non threatening image that tends to attract potential mates.

In other words, there is an underlying language used in courtship. Body language can relay a more powerful message than the spoken language. It can express meekness and harmlessness to attract a mate. It expresses liking and disliking as well as superiority, fear, etc.

4

SECRETS OF BEAUTIFUL WOMEN

SECRET - BEAUTIFUL WOMEN ARE AFRAID TO COME OUT OF THE LADIES ROOM

I have noticed many times during my years of bartending that lots of beautiful women arrive early, long before anyone else even thinks of coming in. This gave me a chance to discuss with them the reasons for these early arrivals.

I remember one beautiful Italian woman in particular. She was about five foot seven inches tall, 110 pounds, and she had dark, curly hair. She combed it half down her back and the other half would curl down in front of her left eye past her cheek. She usually wore a bare lingerie-look top with no bra. You could see just how firm her breasts were because that clingy material was so tight and form fitting under the lace. She had beautiful dark eyes, a perfect nose, and wet pouty lips.

Well, anyway, after a while I knew what she wanted to drink, and I would get it. Then I told her, "I have noticed that lots of beautiful girls come in early. Why do you get here so early? Is it because you think it is going to be so busy later that you'll never get a seat?" She replied, "No, that's not it."

I'm the kind of guy who is never satisfied until I get the real answer. So, I had to wait until she felt comfortable with me before I could get the truth. The truth was that she could get dressed, get in her car, come to the club, and go into the ladies room, but was just too afraid to walk into a club full of strange people. She had to come in before the crowd gets there or else she couldn't come in at all. After that, I started asking the other girls who came in early the same question. They began to admit the same thing. They could not walk into a club full of people, cold.

Getting back to the Italian girl. I guess you want to know what happened with her. This particular club had at least ten bartenders working on the busy nights. A buddy of mine, who was a bartender, liked this girl. He was a good looking guy and about twenty-two years old. She was about twenty-seven or eight, divorced with one child. So, my buddy thought that she might think he was too young for her. I said, "Don't be stupid, she's not going to think you are too young for her." Even this good looking bartender felt he could not approach her because of her beauty and her age. So I said, "Look, during the night I'll tell her about you and find out if she thinks you're too young, okay?" He said, "Well okay, but don't make it too obvious."

As it turns out, she did not think he was too young for her. They got together and had been seeing each other for a year before I lost track of them.

SECRET - WOMEN CAN MAKE UP THEIR MIND, AND MAKE A DECISION, FASTER THAN MEN

I can't even begin to tell you how many times in my twenty plus years of experience, I have watched women accept or reject men in a matter of only a few minutes. They can make a decision about a man within minutes of their first encounter. That is because a woman's brain does not work the same as a man's. Everyone has two hemispheres in their brain. A left hemisphere and a right hemisphere. The man's side of the brain that expresses feelings is less developed. The more developed side of the brain is analytical. Plus, both sides of the brain do not work hand in hand. However, a woman's brain is different. Both sides of her brain work hand in hand, which supposedly enables her to make faster decisions.

As men, we are brought up to be logical. Analyze everything. Look at it from all sides. Take it apart and put it back together. If it is broken, we fix it. If we don't know how to fix it, we will look like a fool to other men. We are supposed to know how everything works in this world. We are supposed to have the right answer for everything. I know I was brought up that way, and I believe we should know how everything works. And if we don't, we should find out, especially if we stand to gain something by finding out.

That is why this book is so valuable to men. Here is a subject men are expected to be experts at. It is our duty to be the aggressive one. We are supposed to know exactly how to initiate a relationship, yet there was no way to learn how, until now.

A woman's brain can generalize. It can take a thought, send it through both hemispheres, and come up with a decision in a MATTER OF MINUTES. That is another reason this book is so important to men. If a man follows the techniques outlined in this book, and studies the surveys, he will know exactly what to do in those crucial first few minutes. Then the woman will be deciding in HIS favor.

SECRET - BEAUTIFUL WOMEN WANT MEN TO TALK ABOUT THEIR FEELINGS

This is a pretty hard thing for us to do. We can't even talk about our feelings with our own mothers, let alone some beautiful stranger. We, again, are not brought up to talk about our feelings. We are brought up to hide our feelings. Ask any dad in this whole country if a boy should cry if he hurts himself. He'll say, "No, crying is for girls, not boys." That is our fathers talking. I know that is how I was brought up, and that is how every other guy in this country (or any other country) has been brought up. I know most of us couldn't cry, even if we wanted to. Imagine Clint Eastwood crying every time someone shot him in his movies. How about the Terminator, although he was a robot, he had a job to do, he did it logically, completed it, and never showed one ounce of emotion. We relate to that so well, but women don't.

You have to learn to communicate with women by sharing your emotions. They want emotional sharing and feelings, and not about our cars or our tools from Sears, either. Try to relate to them through your past relationships, explaining how you are capable of having feelings toward other people.

As men, we have all these emotions and feelings pent up because we don't have an outlet for them. It is a fact that men die younger from the stress we keep inside of us. So, here is a free way of letting out all that stress and pent up emotions. Just tell it to them. They want to hear it anyway. Look at all that money you can save on therapy.

SECRET - BEAUTIFUL WOMEN THINK THEY ARE OLD, NO MATTER WHAT THEIR AGE IS

They are under this delusion that they are old for one reason or another. Men never think they are old. Society never thinks men are old. We just get more DISTINGUISHED. But, society dictates something completely different to women, and they believe it. I have known many beautiful waitresses over the years. They were working for peanuts compared to what they could have been making by modeling or using their looks in a more profitable way, such as TV commercials.

We had a waitress who was tall and beautiful beyond belief. One day I asked her why she was working so hard with such late hours. With her looks, she could be making quite a career for herself as a model. She told me she was too old for that. I asked her, "Well, how old could you be?" She told me she was twenty-one years old, which was "over-the-hill" for that business.

Society dictates to women that after twenty-three, she had better start looking for a husband, because she is starting to pass the age that guys consider prime.

There is only a certain amount of child bearing years for women. So, society puts pressure on the woman to "hurry up" and get started.

SECRET - MOST BEAUTIFUL WOMEN HAVE LESS CHOICES IN MEN THAN AVERAGE LOOKING WOMEN

It sounds like the opposite would be true, but it is not. You would think that beautiful women would have so many choices because every guy wants them.

Well, it's true that everyone wants them, but usually no one feels they are able to get them. Basically, if you are an average looking guy like me, you usually go after average looking girls. You try to stay within your own ball park. Most average looking guys feel the same way. Very rarely will an average looking guy feel that he is good looking enough to satisfy the eye of a beautiful woman. But I know better.

After interviewing so many beautiful women, I began to realize that the most beautiful women were the loneliest women. No one would ask them out because they felt inferior to them.

If a woman is a "10" on a scale of 1 to 10, there aren't many guys who are a "10" or even consider themselves a "10." Even the guys that I knew who were a "10," were afraid of being rejected by other "10" women.

So, beautiful women aren't even approached by great looking men. That is why they are usually home on a friday night by themselves, or out with their girlfriends and NOT with a guy.

The techniques in this book don't only work in nightclubs, they work anywhere. So, the next time you see a beautiful woman in your everyday life experience, and you have read all the techniques in this book, you won't just have to look at her, silently, anymore. You will be able to approach her, say the right thing, and walk away with her phone number. That is the basic idea of this book, to give you more choices in your life.

SECRET - MOST BEAUTIFUL WOMEN HAVE BEEN HURT IN PAST RELATIONSHIPS AND ARE AFRAID OF IT HAPPENING AGAIN

It seems after a man makes a conquest, he is ready to move on, even if it was with a beautiful woman. Women, on the other hand, believe in relationships. They believe in loyalty and trust. Usually when a relationship begins, a woman wants to remain loyal. They sacrifice what they want and replace it with what HE wants. They would do almost anything to please that man. They put the man above anything else.

They start cleaning his house, doing his laundry, washing the dishes, and guys begin to use this against them. Women are trained to do this stuff right from when they are little girls. We are trained to take advantage of this situation right from the time we are little boys. We think, "Well, our mothers did this for us all our lives, so our girlfriend should do it now." So we take it for granted and move on.

I had worked in go-go bars years ago when they used to have male bartenders. Now all you see is female bartenders in these places. I worked about four years in go-go bars, and I learned a lot about these beautiful women. They have some of the biggest problems with relationships. Although they are the same as any other beautiful woman, they are treated differently by men because of what they do for a living.

We think because of the way they dance and slither around up there, almost naked, that they must be the hottest, most promiscuous people on earth. Actually, just the opposite is true. They are more afraid of you than you are of them. They are usually very shy people who are just working for a living, a very good living I might add. Some of those girls can bring home three to four hundred dollars a night. Not bad at all.

This is what motivates them, money not sex. They are not there to meet guys, unless you know what to say to them. Unless you have the insight that this book gives you, basically they want to make their money and get home. We even had to walk them out to their cars at the end of the night. They were so afraid of the guys who came in. Even the guys who went out with these go-go girls would hurt them.

What originally turned their boyfriends on, now turned them off. They did not like their girlfriends dancing any more once they started dating them. They would become jealous and mean to them, if they continued to dance for a living.

I knew some of the most beautiful go-go girls who totally gave up on guys. They were not really homosexual, but they had girlfriends whom they would go out with and have sex with because they just could not stand the pressure men put on them. They would rather have a relationship with another woman than take all the nonsense that men gave them.

SECRET - THE MOST BEAUTIFUL WOMEN THINK THEY ARE NOT BEAUTIFUL AT ALL

This is true. When you see a beautiful woman in your everyday life, you may think, "She is beautiful and sexy, and she knows it." That couldn't be farther from the truth. Women will work hours on their beauty and never be satisfied with it. They are never happy with the way they look, no matter how beautiful WE think they look.

Let us go back to the go-go girls for a second. Most of us can relate to that. These women have to look beautiful from head to toe. They can't hide imperfections with clothes, because they are not wearing very much. And yet they are the most dissatisfied women you can find. They spend hours in the dressing room, making themselves beautiful and fixing their costumes (which they are not going to wear for very long anyway).

But when they come out, to myself and the rest of the guys, they are perfect. To them, everything is wrong. Their hair didn't come out right, their costume does not fit perfect, or their makeup didn't go on right. They think they are a wreck.

The same story holds true for beautiful women everywhere else in the world. When a woman comes to the bar, after spending hours in front of the mirror at home and another hour in the ladies room, she still thinks that she doesn't look right.

I have told so many of these women how beautiful they looked and they would say, "Do you really think so, I think I look terrible." Then I would say, "Okay, what is beautiful to you?" They would say, "Those girls on the cover of Cosmopolitan, now that's beautiful." Little did they know it, but they looked exactly like those girls on the cover of Cosmo. Unfortunately, you could not convince them of that.

Even Jacklyn Smith, one of the worlds true beauties, feels that she has a problem with her nose. When I look at her, I see a beautiful woman. But many times I have read in her interviews that she feels her nose is too thick. So, even the worlds most beautiful women don't consider themselves beautiful.

SECRET - ANY BEAUTIFUL WOMAN IN A NIGHTCLUB IS AVAILABLE, NO MATTER WHO SHE IS WITH OR WHAT SHE IS DOING

Most of the time you see a beautiful woman with her friends or with a boyfriend or waiting for a date to show up. You also see them sitting by themselves. When they are sitting by themselves, you usually think it is okay to approach them. With the proper opening pickup lines outlined in this book, you should have no problem, if they are said sincerely. You will learn more about that in the chapter dedicated to opening pickup lines. Sometimes you will find that when you approach a beautiful woman, she is waiting for her date to meet her there. Don't let this discourage you. Don't just walk away disappointed. This does not mean you are shut out completely. It is just a temporary set back. Continue with the techniques outlined in this book for whatever time you have, until her date gets there. She will not mind talking to you, especially if you are following the procedure of this book. If you are behaving the way women want you to, you can't go wrong. Just go over the chapter on "Interviews With Two Thousand Beautiful Women" to remind yourself just how these beautiful women expect you to behave.

If you really like this woman and don't want her to get away, even though she is meeting a date, you can get her number. Set up a tentative arrangement for lunch sometime when she is not busy, and ask to meet her.

A beautiful woman is always available, even if she has a boyfriend or is meeting a date. She is always open to a man who looks like he knows what he is doing, knows what to say to her, and acts like he knows how to treat her.

You might not have her tonight, but now her number is in your pocket, among many others, for you to pick and choose from.

If you see two women sitting together, and it looks like they are having a great time talking and laughing and having a drink, don't let that prevent you from getting what you want. You must approach the two women at the same time. Use one of the opening pickup lines in this book, but modify it to fit both women. Never exclude the other girl when you approach the one you are interested in. If you do, the other girl will feel that you are just an intrusion. She will feel left out of the fun. She will resent you, because you did not notice her instead of her girlfriend. It brings on many problems that you don't need in a situation like this. If you only pay attention to one girl during the night, and you have to leave to use the men's room (or something), the other girl will start talking you down the minute you are gone. By the time you get back from your trip, you might as well give up because her girlfriend already talked her out of talking with you. Your best bet is to approach the girls with a modified opening pickup line which includes both girls. Don't show either girl special attention. Let both think they are good enough for you. When things seem to be going smoothly, gradually shift your interest over to the one you had your eye on."Quasi-

Let us say you see a table with five or six girls. Let us also say that three are beautiful and two look like

modo" in drag. No matter how bad they might look, when you make your approach include the ugly ones as well. If you have a friend or two, it will help. Especially when you approach a table full of girls. This way all the girls feel they will still be having fun even if you join them. Because there are enough boys and girls, all can have a good time.

Let me give you another technique for approaching a whole table full of beautiful women. This technique will take the pressure off of you, especially if you feel you just can't walk up to the table cold. I used to use this technique, because I didn't have a lot of time when I was working on a busy night. A few buddies of mine were admiring these beautiful girls sitting in a booth, away from the bar. They were having a good time, talking and laughing and having their drinks. When a song was played that they liked, they would come down and dance. Then they would go straight back to their booth. It looked, to my friends, that there was just no way to penetrate this tight group. So, I told them, "look, I'm going to send up the cheapest bottle of champagne we have in the house. It only costs about eleven dollars. I'm going to give it to the waitress with six champagne glasses. I'm going to tell the waitress that this is from us, just because they are the most beautiful girls in the house tonight." I asked the waitress to pour the champagne for the girls, tell them what I said, and point to me when she said it. She did. The beautiful girls raised their glasses and laughed. And we all waved to each other. Now I did not have to approach the table cold. I had already set things in motion. The next chance I got, I approached the table. All the girls were receptive to me. I reinforced the compliment which I had told the waitress to tell them.

I then asked if they wouldn't mind if a few of my friends joined them in a drink. They agreed, and one of my buddies is still going out with one of those girls. Who, by the way, looks almost exactly like Olivia Newton John.

So, for an eleven dollar bottle of champagne, which cost us about three dollars each, the encounter was a success. It was money well spent.

The same rule applies when you are with a buddy or

a couple of guys. Don't predetermine which guy is going to be with which girl when you get to the table. This puts the girls on guard. Just go up with the intention that you are all going to have a good time.

If the women feel that you have pre-planned everything, you are not going to do well. If the women suspect that you have singled them out for sexual reasons, it's over before you even start.

If you had your eye on one particular girl, wait until things are going smoothly before you start focusing your attention on her.

SECRET - BEAUTIFUL WOMEN CAN RELATE TO A MAN NO MATTER HOW OLD OR YOUNG HE MAY BE

There used to be a time when, if you saw a gray haired, older man with a young beautiful girl, you would poke your buddy in the ribs and say, "I wonder how much money he pays her to go out with him." That is not true today at all. Women have no problem relating to much older men. Especially if she thinks he knows how to treat her. By the way, much of this book is devoted to the right way to treat a beautiful woman. But, basically, this book is about "how to get that beautiful woman." Be aware, however, that much of it goes hand in hand.

I believe that the reason a lot of beautiful women are going with older men is partly our faults. As guys, we try to use everything we get our hands on. I'm not saying that's wrong, I'm just saying that is what we do. The women of the 90's are not as naive as they used to be. They are not putting up with it anymore. They are looking for the man with the right answers. Not just anyone that comes by. That is why this book is so important, to help men understand women today.

I used to have a very rich boss who owned a big nightclub in the city. He was about sixty-five years old. His wife was twenty-three and beautiful. She was younger than some of the kids he had with his first wife. For the longest time, I though she was married to him for his money. Although it looked like they related well with each other, I still thought it must be his money she was attracted to. That is what I thought until I found out that this girl's father had ten times the amount of money that my boss had. So, she had all the money she wanted without him. It wasn't the money at all, it was him.

I worked with this beautiful woman once. She had been working about ten years for a big place that could hold approximately four thousand people. It was a banquet facility with a huge nightclub, all in one building. She had done everything there. Finally, she tried her hand at bartending in the lounge during the day. Lots of guys wanted her, but she was fed up with what they wanted her for. Until this older man, not very attractive and carrying a big gut, started bringing her roses when he came in. He used to drink with a group of men at lunchtime. He would then stop in later for a few more drinks just when she was getting off of work. He asked her to join him and a few others for dinner. And so, they started going together. This was one of the most unlikely couples you would ever see. She was tall and beautiful, and he was short, fat, old, and ugly. But, he was treating her the way she wanted to be treated by a man. I could never figure it out. I used to think, he's old and he drinks a lot. How could he take care of a young beautiful woman, especially in bed? That did not seem to make any difference. They got married and had two babies since I last heard from her. I saw them in a restaurant recently, and they still looked happy.

SECRET - DON'T ASSOCIATE THAT BEAUTIFUL WOMAN YOU SEE IN THOSE COMMERCIALS WITH THE ONE YOU MEET IN YOUR EVERYDAY LIFE.

A lot of guys will associate that beautiful woman they see in a nightclub (or restaurant or mall) with that perfect looking woman on television commercials.

The ones in the television commercial seem perfect in every way. They are beautiful from head to toe, or at least they appear to be. They have the perfect mate. She has lots of friends around her, laughing and having a great time. It's a perfect day with the sun shining brightly on her long blond hair and skimpy bikini.

She is usually jumping up and down with her breasts shaking all over the place. Or, she is so happy that she just can't contain herself. She has social status, a great job, and great clothes. Everything is just great. Well, that is why most television commercials last thirty seconds, because that's about how long anyone can afford to keep that up.

The reality is that the beautiful woman that you are looking at in the nightclub (or anywhere else) has the same problems in life that you have. Maybe even more.

I remember this beautiful brunette model that used to come into a place I worked, with about six of her friends. When I first met her, she seemed happy. But, after I got to know her, I found out just how unhappy she was. Although she was modeling and doing commercials, her husband at the time didn't like it. He felt she was spending too much time on her career, and wearing too little clothes doing it. She was a natural beauty, but she felt that wasn't enough. She and her husband separated, and she got breast implants! She took a beautiful, natural body and distorted it with oversized breasts. She did not look good (if you can believe that). She was unhappy and trying too hard. Let me tell you, there was a big difference between how happy and perfect she looked in those television commercials and her real life. And that goes with any other beautiful woman you encounter. Don't associate her with those beautiful, happy women you see on TV.

SECRET - A WOMAN WILL JUDGE HOW YOU WILL MAKE LOVE TO HER BY YOUR FIRST KISS

So, you get to meet this beautiful woman that you have your eye on. You have a couple of drinks and talk and dance. You might suggest breakfast or some other type of activity after the club closes. If she says yes, you will have an opportunity. When it is time to say good night, and you're sure she doesn't want to have sex - just a kiss - make certain you don't overdo it.

Whatever you do at that time will determine whether she will consider having sex with you in the future. If you are very aggressive, unfeeling, impersonal, and you look as though you just want to get right into the sexual act for your own gratification, you might as well forget it. You just blew it with her. There is no sense in getting this far with her just to blow it at this point. The kiss needs to be sensitive and passionate, not too aggressive. It needs to be done with feeling. The kind of kiss that makes her think you are going to make her feelings a number 1 priority. The kind of kiss that tells her you are going to be kind and gentle with her. One that tells her you want her, but you are willing to wait for her to feel secure. And that you understand how important that is for a woman.

I can guarantee that after a kiss like that, she will be thinking about it constantly until the next time you meet.

Besides, what difference does it make. You have all the time in the world. After using my techniques, you will have all the beautiful women you want.

Patience is the key to succeeding with a woman. While you are working on this one, you may already have six others in the bag. So take your time and do it right. Never force the issue. It will come when she is ready.

STUDIES

Shinrigaku Kenkyu 1987 Jun;58(2):91-7
[Self-disclosure patterns of college students and their gender-differences in the patterns].

Enomoto H
Meijo University, Nagoya.

Self-disclosure patterns of adolescents were examined. Subjects (105 male and 159 female college students) were requested to complete the questionnaire on self-disclosure of 11 different aspects of self to four target-persons (father, mother, the best friend of same sex, the best friend of opposite sex). The following results were found. Both male and female showed the highest self-disclosure to the best friend of same sex, while the lowest to father. But sex differences were found in regard to both overall extent and pattern of self-disclosure. Female disclosed significantly more than male, especially to mother. Although male put the focus of self-disclosure on only the best friend of same sex, female put it on both the best friend of same sex and mother. Moreover, the subjects tend to vary the extent of self-disclosure with respect to the category to which each item about the self belonged. There was the interaction among sex, target-persons, and aspects of self.

The point of this study is that women will more easily confide in another woman, such as a best friend. So, if there is any question that you may have regarding how a woman feels about you, the answer could most readily be found through her best friend.

STUDIES

There is a hormone called "oxytocin" that can be created in any one of us through contact with another human being. It is considered to be the "feel good" hormone. Below are studies to illustrated the powerful effect of "oxytocin" followed by a technique that works well.

Oxytocin may mediate the benefits of positive social interaction and emotions.

Uvnas-Moberg K

Department of Physiology and Pharmacology, Karolinska Institute, Stockholm, Sweden.

During breastfeeding or suckling, maternal oxytocin levels are raised by somatosensory stimulation. Oxytocin may, however, also be released by nonnoxious stimuli such as touch, warm temperature etc. In plasma and in cerebrospinal fluid. Consequently, oxytocin may be involved in physiological and behavioral effects induced by social interaction in a more general context. ~ Positive social interactions have been related to health-promoting effects. Oxytocin released in response to social stimuli may be part of a neuroendocrine substrate which underlies the benefits of positive social experiences. Such processes may in addition explain the health-promoting effects of certain alternative therapies. Because of the special properties of oxytocin, including the fact that it can become conditioned to psychological state or imagery, oxytocin may also mediate the benefits attributed to therapies such as hypnosis or meditation.

STUDIES

****

Ann N Y Acad Sci 1997 Jan 15;807:146-63

Physiological and endocrine effects of social contact.

Uvnas-Moberg K
Department of Physiology and Pharmacology, Karolinska Institute, Stockholm, Sweden.

Nonnoxious sensory stimulation associated with friendly social interaction induces a psychophysiological response pattern involving sedation, relaxation, decreased sympathoadrenal activity, and increased vagal nerve tone and thereby an endocrine and metabolic pattern favoring the storage of nutrients and growth. It is suggested that oxytocin released from parvocellular neurons in the paraventricular nucleus (PVN) in response to nonnoxious stimulation integrates this response pattern at the hypothalamic level. The response pattern just described characterized by calm, relaxation, and anabolic metabolism could be regarded as an antithesis to the well known fight-flight response in which mental activation, locomotor activity, and catabolic metabolism are expressed. Furthermore, the health-promoting aspect of friendly and supportive relationships might be a consequence of repetitive exposure to nonnoxious sensory stimulation causing the physiological endocrine and behavioral changes just described.

****

STUDIES

Indian J Med Sci 1995 Nov;49(11):261-6

Oxytocin induces intimate behaviors.

Rao GM
Great Al-Fateh University of Medical Sciences, Tripoli, Libya

After decades of classic research on its secretion from the neurohypophysis and its potential effects in the uterus and the gland, oxytocin has, in the last 15 years, been proven to be centrally distributed neuropeptide with broad spectrum of behavioral effects. Of particular interest are reports of potent effects of oxytocin on many reproductive and social behaviors such as maternal behavior, female sexual receptivity (lordosis). The nonapeptides promote a large number of key behavioral interactions between conspecifics than any other class of neuropeptides. Nonapeptides may trigger the appropriate intraspecific affiliative behavior under broad range of reproductive and social conditions.

The idea of this technique is to stimulate the hormone "Oxytocin" in the girl you are trying to get a date from. In order to stimulate this hormone, one must touch the other party. Although there is no proper way to touch a women you just met, it is acceptable to shake her hand. You can take this one step further by reading her palm. By holding her hand and reading her palm, you are creating this same hormone and producing that initial chemistry that is so important between male and female. By touching in this manner the hormone "Oxytocin" will create a sense of bonding for the woman. I realize you may not know how to read palms so let me give you a brief overview. The general idea of palm reading, basically, is the reading of lines in the hand. In the palm of the hand there is a "lifeline" which is the line that is created by the thumb muscle. There is a "fateline" that runs straight down the middle of the palm. And there is a "heartline" which is the deep line that runs almost horizontally, right below the pinkie, ring and middle fingers. These are the basic feature lines of the palm. Remember, the object of this technique is to give you an excuse to hold her hand so that the hormone "oxytocin" will become active in her. If you must, buy a book on palm reading and incorporate all the positive points from the book into your reading. For example, her "lifeline" indicates to you that she is going to have a long life, or her "fateline" indicates that she is going to encounter great prosperity in her life, etc. As you are elaborating on her good fortune, remember to gently stroke the lines of her palm with your finger in a soothing and gentle manner.

5

INTERVIEWS WITH TWO THOUSAND BEAUTIFUL WOMEN

Of all the chapters in this book, I feel this is probably the most important. Of all my twenty-three years experience of dealing with beautiful women, this chapter is the most insightful. I'm glad I waited until now to write this book. Had I written it ten years ago, I would have had to change it or write a new book today. In the twenty-three years that I've been in this business, the last ten years has changed in many ways, especially as women are concerned. In the last ten years, women have changed drastically with regard to their position in society. They are not the same women we knew ten years ago. The winds of change and awareness have blown across this country, and we had better be aware of these changes and what to do about them.

Of the thousands of beautiful women I had interviewed over the years, I have found out a lot of information which I will share with you.

There was a time when you could say almost anything when you were trying to get a beautiful woman. But today, what you say and what you do matter more than anything else. We are now dealing with a more intelligent breed of woman than we were ten years ago. But there is definitely a way to deal with it. I just needed twenty-three years, and a few thousand interviews, to figure it out.

I wanted to find out exactly what made these beautiful women tick. With all this beauty in the world, as a man, I wanted to know how to get it. Now that I know, I wanted to tell you the secrets.

I started interviewing every beautiful woman that came into the clubs I worked at. Every time I saw a beautiful woman, no matter where she was sitting, I would approach her with my interview and ask her if she wouldn't mind completing it. Then I would discuss it further with her to get as much information as I possibly could. After about the first thousand interviews, I started to get an understanding about these beautiful women that we will elaborate on during this chapter.

At this point, I was positive about what these beautiful women wanted from men when they were in nightclubs. So I decided to broaden my interviews with beautiful women outside of this environment. I wanted to know if beautiful women felt the same when they were in the laundromat, at a restaurant, at their jobs, or wherever they were.

I had a friend who was an executive for a big company. One day I stopped in to see him. There must have been one hundred beautiful looking receptionists and secretaries working there. I asked him if I could interview them for my book. He agreed, so I selected about forty whom I thought were the most beautiful. After interviewing them, I found out that they felt the same way the beautiful women in the nightclubs felt. So I then interviewed women in laundromats, malls, restaurants, and anyplace I saw one. I came out with some remarkable discoveries which I will share with you. I never stopped interviewing beautiful women in nightclubs. So when I reached over two thousand interviews, I decided I was ready to hand the information over to you.

I thought, how are you going to get a feel for these interviews if you don't read them for yourself. I don't want to just analyze them for you. I want you to read them. I can't put over two thousand interviews into this book, however. I was trying to decide just how many interviews I can put into my book, so that you can start to get a feel for what these beautiful women want. I decided on about forty interviews. This would be a good amount for someone to realize what the beautiful women of today want from us.

I didn't put in the best or worst. I picked the ones that reflect the average responses I got from the thousands I had.

As you read these interviews, picture yourself walking up to a beautiful woman and basically asking her what it would take to pick her up. That is exactly what I did in essence. So try to imagine the beautiful woman you saw in the mall or the restaurant or at the nightclub. And imagine yourself asking her the questions on the interview. Because these interviews were taken from beautiful women, and these are their answers, I left the interviews exactly the way they were written.

INTERVIEW FOR WOMEN

THANK YOU FOR TAKING THE TIME TO FILL OUT THIS SURVEY. I AM CURRENTLY DOING RESEARCH FOR A NEW BOOK AND ALL INFORMATION RECEIVED IS ANONYMOUS.

1. What top 3 attributes do you expect men to have when he approaches you.

- [ ] good manners
- [x] neatly dressed
- [x] pleasant smile
- [x] nice personality
- [ ] congeniality
- [ ] honesty
- [ ] affectionate
- [ ] friendly
- [ ] sociability

2. How should he be dressed?

- [ ] dressed up
- [ ] dressed down
- [ ] extra casual
- [x] does not matter

3. Should he be smiling?

- [x] yes
- [ ] no

4. What style of hair do you like?

- [ ] long
- [x] short
- [ ] pony tail
- [ ] bald

5. Do you like a man that you just met to be:

- [ ] serious
- [ ] comical
- [x] romantic

6. What is the first thing a man could say to you that would make you feel good?

He noticed you out of all the other women in the room

7. What was the nicest, unusual or funniest line a man has ever told you? I can't stop thinking about you.

8. What was the nicest compliment a man has ever paid you?
You have great legs.

9. What is the biggest turn off about a man in your opinion?
Dirty fingernails, bad teeth & Chauvinistic

10. What would be the worst thing a man could say, when he first approaches you? What's a nice girl like you doing here.

11. What is the first thing you look at on a man?

- O hair
- O height
- O muscles
- O buns
- O eyes
- O weight
- ☑ other hands & arms

INTERVIEW FOR WOMEN

THANK YOU FOR TAKING THE TIME TO FILL OUT THIS SURVEY. I AM CURRENTLY DOING RESEARCH FOR A NEW BOOK AND ALL INFORMATION RECEIVED IS ANONYMOUS.

1. What top 3 attributes do you expect men to have when he approaches you.

 - O good manners
 - O neatly dressed
 - O pleasant smile
 - O nice personality
 - O congeniality
 - O honesty
 - O affectionate
 - O friendly
 - O sociability

2. How should he be dressed?

 - O dressed up
 - O dressed down
 - O extra casual
 - O does not matter

3. Should he be smiling?

 - O yes
 - O no

4. What style of hair do you like?

 - O long
 - O short
 - O pony tail
 - O bald

5. Do you like a man that you just met to be:

 - O serious
 - O comical
 - O romantic

6. What is the first thing a man could say to you that would make you feel good? You look beautiful!

7. What was the nicest, unusual or funniest line a man has ever told you?

that I am beautiful when I know I look horrible — and he really means it!

8. What was the nicest compliment a man has ever paid you?

I have nice eyes / or personality

9. What is the biggest turn off about a man in your opinion?

when he is full of himself

10. What would be the worst thing a man could say, when he first approaches you?

any usual line used too much!

11. What is the first thing you look at on a man?

- ☐ hair
- ☐ height
- ☐ muscles
- ☐ buns
- ☐ eyes
- ☐ weight
- ☒ other

Whether he is smiling and looks like he is a fun person!

INTERVIEW FOR WOMEN

THANK YOU FOR TAKING THE TIME TO FILL OUT THIS SURVEY. I AM CURRENTLY DOING RESEARCH FOR A NEW BOOK AND ALL INFORMATION RECEIVED IS ANONYMOUS.

1. What top 3 attributes do you expect men to have when he approaches you.

   X good manners
   O neatly dressed
   O pleasant smile
   O nice personality
   O congeniality
   X honesty
   O affectionate
   O friendly
   X sociability

2. How should he be dressed?

   O dressed up
   O dressed down
   O extra casual
   X does not matter

3. Should he be smiling?

   X yes
   O no

4. What style of hair do you like?

   O long
   O short
   X pony tail
   O bald

5. Do you like a man that you just met to be:

   O serious
   X comical
   O romantic

6. What is the first thing a man could say to you that would make you feel good? your beautiful

7. What was the nicest, unusual or funniest line a man has ever told you? You make me melt.

8. What was the nicest compliment a man has ever paid you?
~~[illegible]~~ I have nice eyes ~~[illegible]~~

9. What is the biggest turn off about a man in your opinion?
~~[illegible]~~ Show off

10. What would be the worst thing a man could say, when he first approaches you? A stupid old line you probably heard 10 million times

11. What is the first thing you look at on a man?

- O hair
- O height
- O muscles
- O buns
- X eyes
- O weight
- O other

INTERVIEW FOR WOMEN

THANK YOU FOR TAKING THE TIME TO FILL OUT THIS SURVEY. I AM CURRENTLY DOING RESEARCH FOR A NEW BOOK AND ALL INFORMATION RECEIVED IS ANONYMOUS.

1. What top 3 attributes do you expect men to have when he approaches you.

   - O good manners
   - O neatly dressed
   - O pleasant smile
   - ☑ nice personality
   - O congeniality
   - ☑ honesty
   - O affectionate
   - ☑ friendly
   - O sociability

2. How should he be dressed?

   - O dressed up
   - O dressed down
   - O extra casual
   - ☑ does not matter (but clean)

3. Should he be smiling?

   - ☑ yes
   - O no

4. What style of hair do you like?

   - ☑ long
   - O short
   - O pony tail
   - O bald

5. Do you like a man that you just met to be:

   - O serious
   - ☑ comical
   - O romantic

6. What is the first thing a man could say to you that would make you feel good?

   I love your eyes
   you look like you are having a pleasant time, may I join you?

7. What was the nicest, unusual or funniest line a man has ever told you?

I was very closed to the world - you have opened me up to a whole range of new things.

8. What was the nicest compliment a man has ever paid you?

you have a Playboy body in miniature

9. What is the biggest turn off about a man in your opinion?

talks about sex too much.

10. What would be the worst thing a man could say, when he first approaches you?

"can I buy you a drink" or
"do you live around here"

11. What is the first thing you look at on a man?

- [x] hair
- [x] height
- [x] muscles
- [x] buns
- [x] eyes
- [x] weight
- [x] other

INTERVIEW FOR WOMEN

THANK YOU FOR TAKING THE TIME TO FILL OUT THIS SURVEY. I AM CURRENTLY DOING RESEARCH FOR A NEW BOOK AND ALL INFORMATION RECEIVED IS ANONYMOUS.

1. What top 3 attributes do you expect men to have when he approaches you.

   - ☒ good manners
   - ☒ neatly dressed
   - ☒ pleasant smile
   - O nice personality
   - O congeniality
   - O honesty
   - O affectionate
   - O friendly
   - O sociability

2. How should he be dressed?

   - O dressed up
   - O dressed down
   - O extra casual
   - ☒ does not matter

3. Should he be smiling?

   - ☒ yes
   - O no

4. What style of hair do you like?

   - ☒ long
   - O short
   - O pony tail
   - O bald

5. Do you like a man that you just met to be:

   - O serious
   - ☒ comical
   - O romantic

6. What is the first thing a man could say to you that would make you feel good?

   You look like your having a good time

7. What was the nicest, unusual or funniest line a man has ever told you?

I played this song for you.

8. What was the nicest compliment a man has ever paid you?

You are so nice to be around.

9. What is the biggest turn off about a man in your opinion?

Loud and Violent

10. What would be the worst thing a man could say, when he first approaches you?

~~Something~~ Some old line that my grandfather might have told my grandmother.

11. What is the first thing you look at on a man?

- ☐ hair
- ☐ height
- ☐ muscles
- ☐ buns
- ☑ eyes
- ☐ weight
- ☐ other

INTERVIEW FOR WOMEN

THANK YOU FOR TAKING THE TIME TO FILL OUT THIS SURVEY. I AM CURRENTLY DOING RESEARCH FOR A NEW BOOK AND ALL INFORMATION RECEIVED IS ANONYMOUS.

1. What top 3 attributes do you expect men to have when he approaches you.

- O good manners
- O neatly dressed
- O pleasant smile
- O nice personality
- O congeniality
- O honesty
- O affectionate
- O friendly
- O sociability

2. How should he be dressed?

- O dressed up
- O dressed down
- O ~~extra~~ casual
- O does not matter

3. Should he be smiling?

- O yes
- O no

4. What style of hair do you like?

- O long
- O short
- O pony tail
- O bald

5. Do you like a man that you just met to be:

- O serious
- O comical
- O romantic

6. What is the first thing a man could say to you that would make you fuel good?

referencing about looks

7. What was the nicest, unusual or funniest line a man has ever told you? I'd like to marry a girl like you & buy her a house on the oceanfront & live with her forever.

8. What was the nicest compliment a man has ever paid you?

I'd like you to be the mother of my children.

9. What is the biggest turn off about a man in your opinion?

being aggressively overwhelming

10. What would be the worst thing a man could say, when he first approaches you?

haven't I met you someplace before?

11. What is the first thing you look at on a man?

- O hair
- (O) height (circled)
- O muscles
- O buns
- (O) eyes (circled)
- O weight
- O other

INTERVIEW FOR WOMEN

THANK YOU FOR TAKING THE TIME TO FILL OUT THIS SURVEY. I AM CURRENTLY DOING RESEARCH FOR A NEW BOOK AND ALL INFORMATION RECEIVED IS ANONYMOUS.

1. What top 3 attributes do you expect men to have when he approaches you.

   ☑ good manners ☑ honesty
   O neatly dressed O affectionate
   O pleasant smile O friendly
   ☑ nice personality O sociability
   O congeniality

2. How should he be dressed?

   O dressed up
   ☑ dressed down
   O extra casual
   O does not matter

3. Should he be smiling?

   ☑ yes
   O no

4. What style of hair do you like?

   O long
   ☑ short
   O pony tail
   O bald

5. Do you like a man that you just met to be:

   O serious
   ☑ comical
   O romantic

6. What is the first thing a man could say to you that would make you feel good? Sincere Compliment

7. What was the nicest, unusual or funniest line a man has ever told you?

HAVE NOT HEAR 1 YET.

8. What was the nicest compliment a man has ever paid you?

THAT I HANDLE MYSELF WELL IN All situations

9. What is the biggest turn off about a man in your opinion?

BAD TEETH BAD MANNERS BAD BREATH.

10. What would be the worst thing a man could say, when he first approaches you?

Anything that sounds like an ORDER, OR line

11. What is the first thing you look at on a man?

- 0 hair
- 0 height
- 0 muscles
- 0 buns
- ✓ eyes
- 0 weight
- 0 other

INTERVIEW FOR WOMEN

THANK YOU FOR TAKING THE TIME TO FILL OUT THIS SURVEY. I AM CURRENTLY DOING RESEARCH FOR A NEW BOOK AND ALL INFORMATION RECEIVED IS ANONYMOUS.

1. What top 3 attributes do you expect men to have when he approaches you.

- ☐ good manners
- ☐ neatly dressed
- ☐ pleasant smile
- ☒ nice personality
- ☐ congeniality
- ☒ honesty
- ☐ affectionate
- ☐ friendly
- ☒ sociability

2. How should he be dressed?

- ☐ dressed up
- ☐ dressed down
- ☒ extra casual
- ☐ does not matter

3. Should he be smiling?

- ☒ yes
- ☐ no

4. What style of hair do you like?

- ☐ long
- ☐ short
- ☒ pony tail
- ☐ bald

5. Do you like a man that you just met to be:

- ☐ serious
- ☒ comical
- ☐ romantic

6. What is the first thing a man could say to you that would make you feel good?

"HOW ARE YOU DOING?" (WITH SINCERITY)

7. What was the nicest, unusual or funniest line a man has ever told you?

HE TOLD ME THAT I COULD GO AND LIVE THE WILD THAT I HAD MISSED IN MY YOUNGER YEARS AND HE STILL BE WAITING FOR ME WHEN I WAS FINISHED.

8. What was the nicest compliment a man has ever paid you?

"YOU HAVE A NICE SMILE."

9. What is the biggest turn off about a man in your opinion?

INSENSITIVITY

10. What is the worst thing a man has ever said to you?

"DID EVERYTHING COME OUT ALRIGHT?" (AFTER A TRIP TO THE LADIES' ROOM.)

11. What is the first thing you look on a man?

- [ ] hair
- [ ] height
- [ ] muscles
- [ ] buns
- [x] eyes
- [ ] weight
- [ ] other

INTERVIEW FOR WOMEN

THANK YOU FOR TAKING THE TIME TO FILL OUT THIS SURVEY. I AM CURRENTLY DOING RESEARCH FOR A NEW BOOK AND ALL INFORMATION RECEIVED IS ANONYMOUS.

1. What top 3 attributes do you expect men to have when he approaches you.

- ● good manners
- O neatly dressed
- O pleasant smile
- ● nice personality
- O congeniality
- ● honesty
- O affectionate
- O friendly
- O sociability

2. How should he be dressed?

- O dressed up
- O dressed down
- O extra casual
- ● does not matter

3. Should he be smiling?

- ● yes
- O no

4. What style of hair do you like?

- O long
- ● short
- O pony tail
- O bald

5. Do you like a man that you just met to be:

- O serious
- ● comical
- O romantic

6. What is the first thing a man could say to you that would make you feel good?

That he found me attractive and he'd like to see me & get to know me better.

7. What was the nicest, unusual or funniest line a man has ever told you? He asked me out - I told him I had a boyfriend and he said he didn't want to take him out - just me.

8. What was the nicest compliment a man has ever paid you?

I want to spend my life with you.

9. What is the biggest turn off about a man in your opinion?

Someone who is too pushy.

10. What would be the worst thing a man could say, when he first approaches you?

Any old line like "Do you come here often?"

11. What is the first thing you look at on a man?

- ■ hair
- ☐ height
- ☐ muscles
- ☐ buns
- ☐ eyes
- ☐ weight
- ☐ other

94

INTERVIEW FOR WOMEN

THANK YOU FOR TAKING THE TIME TO FILL OUT THIS SURVEY. I AM CURRENTLY DOING RESEARCH FOR A NEW BOOK AND ALL INFORMATION RECEIVED IS ANONYMOUS.

1. What top 3 attributes do you expect men to have when he approaches you.

   X good manners
   O neatly dressed
   X pleasant smile
   O nice personality
   O congeniality
   O honesty
   O affectionate
   X friendly
   O sociability

2. How should he be dressed?

   O dressed up
   O dressed down
   O extra casual
   X does not matter

3. Should he be smiling?

   X yes
   O no

4. What style of hair do you like?

   O long
   X short
   O pony tail
   O bald

5. Do you like a man that you just met to be:

   O serious
   X comical
   O romantic

6. What is the first thing a man could say to you that would make you feel good?

   Some kind of complimentary statement about why he approached me.

7. What was the nicest, unusual or funniest line a man has ever told you?

I feel like we've been here before as if I've known you all my life.

8. What was the nicest compliment a man has ever paid you?

Not only are you attractive but also intelligent & sensitive.

9. What is the biggest turn off about a man in your opinion?

Expecting sex or sexual responsiveness on a first or second meeting.

10. What would be the worst thing a man could say, when he first approaches you?

your bust is really kick'n

(yuk!)

11. What is the first thing you look at on a man?

- ☐ hair
- ☐ height
- ☐ muscles
- ☐ buns
- ☒ eyes
- ☐ weight
- ☐ other

INTERVIEW FOR WOMEN

THANK YOU FOR TAKING THE TIME TO FILL OUT THIS SURVEY. I AM CURRENTLY DOING RESEARCH FOR A NEW BOOK AND ALL INFORMATION RECEIVED IS ANONYMOUS.

1. What top 3 attributes do you expect men to have when he approaches you.

   - ● good manners
   - O neatly dressed
   - O pleasant smile
   - ● nice personality
   - O congeniality
   - O honesty
   - O affectionate
   - ● friendly
   - O sociability

2. How should he be dressed?

   - O dressed up
   - O dressed down
   - O extra casual
   - ● does not matter

3. Should he be smiling?

   - ● yes
   - O no

4. What style of hair do you like?

   - ● long
   - O short
   - ● pony tail
   - O bald

5. Do you like a man that you just met to be:

   - O serious
   - ● comical
   - O romantic

6. What is the first thing a man could say to you that would make you feel good?

   Hi- how are you!?, Youve got a great smile!

7. What was the nicest, unusual or funniest line a man has ever told you?

"Wow! how tall ARE you?"

8. What was the nicest compliment a man has ever paid you? Your smile is so nice, I can even see it in the dark - and your entire face just lights up!

9. What is the biggest turn off about a man in your opinion? Matirialism

10. What is the worst thing a man has ever said to you? "You know. I'm dying to get in your pants" - (I said - NO THANKS, I already have one asshole in there!)

11. What is the first thing you look on a man?

- ☐ hair
- ☐ height
- ☐ muscles
- ☐ buns
- ☐ eyes
- ☐ weight
- ■ other Smile - teeth

INTERVIEW FOR WOMEN

THANK YOU FOR TAKING THE TIME TO FILL OUT THIS SURVEY. I AM CURRENTLY DOING RESEARCH FOR A NEW BOOK AND ALL INFORMATION RECEIVED IS ANONYMOUS.

1. What top 3 attributes do you expect men to have when he approaches you.

   - [x] good manners
   - [ ] neatly dressed
   - [ ] pleasant smile
   - [x] nice personality
   - [ ] congeniality
   - [ ] honesty
   - [ ] affectionate
   - [ ] friendly
   - [x] sociability

2. How should he be dressed?

   - [ ] dressed up
   - [ ] dressed down
   - [ ] extra casual
   - [x] does not matter

3. Should he be smiling?

   - [x] yes
   - [ ] no

4. What style of hair do you like?

   - [ ] long
   - [x] short
   - [ ] pony tail
   - [ ] bald

5. Do you like a man that you just met to be:

   - [x] serious
   - [x] comical
   - [ ] romantic

   combination of both - depends on topic of conversation

6. What is the first thing a man could say to you that would make you feel good?

   Depends on the circumstance & the meeting place. Something very regular though & natural. Anything that sounds phony is a turn off.

7. What was the nicest, unusual or funniest line a man has ever told you?

"Didn't we go to different schools at the same time?"

8. What was the nicest compliment a man has ever paid you? Whether it was true or not — someone said I was an angel & the perfect woman.

9. What is the biggest turn off about a man in your opinion?

A general obnoxious attitude & a big ego - without reason to have one.

10. What is the worst thing a man has ever said to you?

I'm too much of a lady to repeat!

11. What is the first thing you look on a man?

- O hair
- O height
- O muscles
- O buns
- O eyes
- O weight
- X other

Overall appearance & the way he's dressed.

INTERVIEW FOR WOMEN

THANK YOU FOR TAKING THE TIME TO FILL OUT THIS SURVEY. I AM CURRENTLY DOING RESEARCH FOR A NEW BOOK AND ALL INFORMATION RECEIVED IS ANONYMOUS.

1. What top 3 attributes do you expect men to have when he approaches you.

- ✓ good manners
- O neatly dressed
- ✓ pleasant smile
- ✓ nice personality
- O congeniality
- O honesty
- O affectionate
- O friendly
- O sociability

2. How should he be dressed?

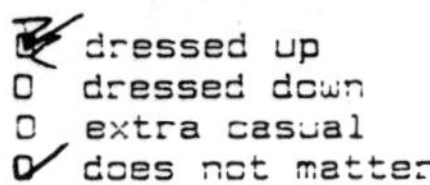

- O dressed up
- O dressed down
- O extra casual
- ✓ does not matter

3. Should he be smiling?

- ✓ yes
- O no

4. What style of hair do you like?

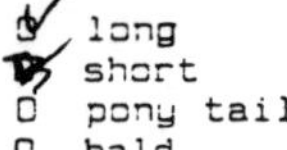

- ✓ long
- ✓ short
- O pony tail
- O bald

5. Do you like a man that you just met to be:

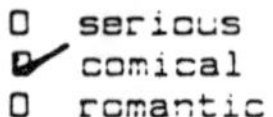

- O serious
- ✓ comical
- O romantic

6. What is the first thing a man could say to you that would make you feel good?

something about the way I look.

7. What was the nicest, unusual or funniest line a man has ever told you?

You don't look old enough to drink.

8. What was the nicest compliment a man has ever paid you?

That I looked like a model.

9. What is the biggest turn off about a man in your opinion?

When he ~~tells you~~ exaggerates his success. & has an attitude

10. What is the worst thing a man has ever said to you?

I like women ~~wi~~ with big boobs

11. What is the first thing you look on a man?

- ☒ hair
- ☐ height
- ☐ muscles
- ☐ buns
- ☐ eyes
- ☐ weight
- ☑ other (hands)

INTERVIEW FOR WOMEN

THANK YOU FOR TAKING THE TIME TO FILL OUT THIS SURVEY. I AM CURRENTLY DOING RESEARCH FOR A NEW BOOK AND ALL INFORMATION RECEIVED IS ANONYMOUS.

1. What top 3 attributes do you expect men to have when he approaches you.

   - O good manners
   - ☑ neatly dressed
   - ☑ pleasant smile
   - O nice personality
   - O congeniality
   - O honesty
   - O affectionate
   - O friendly
   - ☑ sociability

2. How should he be dressed?

   - O dressed up
   - O dressed down
   - O extra casual
   - ☑ does not matter

3. Should he be smiling?

   - ☑ yes
   - O no

4. What style of hair do you like?

   - O long
   - ☑ short
   - O pony tail
   - O bald

5. Do you like a man that you just met to be:

   - O serious
   - O comical
   - ☑ romantic

6. What is the first thing a man could say to you that would make you feel good?

   a nice comment about a feature or style of clothes

7. What was the nicest, unusual or funniest line a man has ever told you?

Can't remember!

8. What was the nicest compliment a man has ever paid you?

You should be a model

9. What is the biggest turn off about a man in your opinion?

dirty looks, hair, clothes etc.

10. What is the worst thing a man has ever said to you?

You think you could handle a 26 yr. old? (I was 18)

11. What is the first thing you look on a man?

- O hair
- O height
- O muscles
- O buns
- O eyes
- X weight
- O other

INTERVIEW FOR WOMEN

THANK YOU FOR TAKING THE TIME TO FILL OUT THIS SURVEY. I AM CURRENTLY DOING RESEARCH FOR A NEW BOOK AND ALL INFORMATION RECEIVED IS ANONYMOUS.

1. What top 3 attributes do you expect men to have when he approaches you.

   - [ ] good manners
   - [ ] neatly dressed
   - [x] pleasant smile
   - [ ] nice personality
   - [ ] congeniality
   - [x] honesty
   - [ ] affectionate
   - [x] friendly
   - [ ] sociability

2. How should he be dressed?

   - [ ] dressed up
   - [ ] dressed down
   - [ ] extra casual
   - [x] does not matter

3. Should he be smiling?

   - [x] yes
   - [ ] no

4. What style of hair do you like?

   - [ ] long
   - [x] short
   - [ ] pony tail
   - [ ] bald

5. Do you like a man that you just met to be:

   - [x] serious
   - [ ] comical
   - [ ] romantic

6. What is the first thing a man could say to you that would make you feel good?

   "I couldn't help noticing you..."

7. What was the nicest, unusual or funniest line a man has ever told you? "What's an angel like you doing so far from heaven?"

8. What was the nicest compliment a man has ever paid you? You are the most "complete woman" I have ever met.

9. What is the biggest turn off about a man in your opinion? weakness

10. What is the worst thing a man has ever said to you? You're lucky I stopped to talk to you.

11. What is the first thing you look on a man?

- ☐ hair
- ☐ height
- ☐ muscles
- ☐ buns
- ☑ eyes
- ☐ weight
- ☐ other

INTERVIEW FOR WOMEN

THANK YOU FOR TAKING THE TIME TO FILL OUT THIS SURVEY. I AM CURRENTLY DOING RESEARCH FOR A NEW BOOK AND ALL INFORMATION RECEIVED IS ANONYMOUS.

1. What top 3 attributes do you expect men to have when he approaches you.

- ☐ good manners
- ☐ neatly dressed
- ☒ pleasant smile
- ☒ nice personality
- ☐ congeniality
- ☐ honesty
- ☐ affectionate
- ☒ friendly
- ☐ sociability

2. How should he be dressed?

- ☒ dressed up
- ☐ dressed down
- ☐ extra casual
- ☐ does not matter

3. Should he be smiling?

- ☒ yes
- ☐ no

4. What style of hair do you like?

- ☐ long
- ☒ short
- ☐ pony tail
- ☐ bald

5. Do you like a man that you just met to be:

- ☐ serious
- ☐ comical
- ☒ romantic

6. What is the first thing a man could say to you that would make you feel good?

I saw you with your friends and I was wondering if I could talk with you because you really stand out of the crowd. And I would love to take you out to dinner

7. What was the nicest, unusual or funniest line a man has ever told you?

The reason I liked you because you have the nicest butt.

8. What was the nicest compliment a man has ever paid you?

Now That I have talked with you I realize you are not only Beatiful but very intelligent

9. What is the biggest turn off about a man in your opinion?

Not Being themselfes showing off or Bragging

10. What is the worst thing a man has ever said to you?

I think you are real pretty how about me and you haveing a one nighter

11. What is the first thing you look on a man?

- [ ] hair
- [ ] height
- [ ] muscles
- [ ] buns
- [x] eyes
- [ ] weight
- [ ] other

INTERVIEW FOR WOMEN

THANK YOU FOR TAKING THE TIME TO FILL OUT THIS SURVEY. I AM CURRENTLY DOING RESEARCH FOR A NEW BOOK AND ALL INFORMATION RECEIVED IS ANONYMOUS.

1. What top 3 attributes do you expect men to have when he approaches you.

   O good manners
   O neatly dressed
   O pleasant smile
   O nice personality
   O congeniality
   O honesty
   O affectionate
   O friendly
   O sociability

2. How should he be dressed?

   O dressed up
   O dressed down
   O extra casual
   O does not matter

3. Should he be smiling?

   O yes
   O no

4. What style of hair do you like?

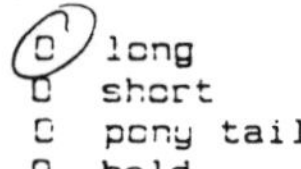

   O long
   O short
   O pony tail
   O bald

5. Do you like a man that you just met to be:

   O serious
   O comical
   O romantic

6. What is the first thing a man could say to you that would make you feel good?

   something about the way I look

7. What was the nicest, unusual or funniest line a man has ever told you?

~~[illegible]~~ Come here, I want to whisper something ~~to~~ 'in your ~~[illegible]~~ ear

8. What was the nicest compliment a man has ever paid you?

~~[illegible]~~ my unpretencious personality

9. What is the biggest turn off about a man in your opinion?

something about how hot he is & how everyone wants him.

10. What is the worst thing a man has ever said to you?

Do I know you from somewhere? Then why are you staring at me?

11. What is the first thing you look on a man?

- (O) hair
- O height
- O muscles
- O buns
- O eyes
- O weight
- O other

INTERVIEW FOR WOMEN

THANK YOU FOR TAKING THE TIME TO FILL OUT THIS SURVEY. I AM CURRENTLY DOING RESEARCH FOR A NEW BOOK AND ALL INFORMATION RECEIVED IS ANONYMOUS.

1. What top 3 attributes do you expect men to have when he approaches you.

- [x] good manners
- [x] neatly dressed
- [ ] pleasant smile
- [ ] nice personality
- [ ] congeniality
- [ ] honesty
- [x] affectionate
- [ ] friendly
- [ ] sociability

2. How should he be dressed?

- [ ] dressed up
- [ ] dressed down
- [ ] extra casual
- [x] does not matter

3. Should he be smiling?

- [x] ~~yes~~
- [ ] no

4. What style of hair do you like?

- [ ] long
- [x] short
- [ ] pony tail
- [ ] bald

5. Do you like a man that you just met to be:

- [ ] serious
- [x] comical
- [ ] romantic

6. What is the first thing a man could say to you that would make you feel good?

I'm sorry, I thought you were Cindy Crawford -

7. What was the nicest, unusual or <u>funniest</u> line a man has ever told you?
WATTA SAY YOU Come home with me and have A threesome with my wife & I?

8. What was the nicest compliment a man has ever paid you?
You have the most breathtalcing eyes

9. What is the biggest turn off about a man in your opinion?
food in his teeth

10. What would be the worst thing a man could say, when he first approaches you?
So you live Around here often- burp!

11. What is the first thing you look at on a man?

- ☐ hair
- ☐ height
- ☐ muscles
- ☐ buns
- ☒ eyes
- ☐ weight
- ☐ other

INTERVIEW FOR WOMEN

THANK YOU FOR TAKING THE TIME TO FILL OUT THIS SURVEY. I AM CURRENTLY DOING RESEARCH FOR A NEW BOOK AND ALL INFORMATION RECEIVED IS ANONYMOUS.

1. What top 3 attributes do you expect men to have when he approaches you.

X	good manners	X	honesty
X	neatly dressed	O	affectionate
O	pleasant smile	O	friendly
O	nice personality	O	sociability
O	congeniality		

2. How should he be dressed?

O dressed up
O dressed down
O extra casual
X does not matter

3. Should he be smiling?

X yes
O no

4. What style of hair do you like?

O long
X short
O pony tail
O bald

5. Do you like a man that you just met to be:

X serious
X comical
O romantic

6. What is the first thing a man could say to you that would make you feel good?

you look real nice

7. What was the nicest, unusual or funniest line a man has ever told you?

take that ring off because I'm going to marry you

8. What was the nicest compliment a man has ever paid you?

you smile is beautiful

9. What is the biggest turn off about a man in your opinion?

bad breath & dirty body

10. What would be the worst thing a man could say, when he first approaches you?

hey baby whats your name

11. What is the first thing you look at on a man?

- O hair
- O height
- O muscles
- O buns
- O eyes
- O weight
- O other

all above

INTERVIEW FOR WOMEN

THANK YOU FOR TAKING THE TIME TO FILL OUT THIS SURVEY. I AM CURRENTLY DOING RESEARCH FOR A NEW BOOK AND ALL INFORMATION RECEIVED IS ANONYMOUS.

1. What top 3 attributes do you expect men to have when he approaches you.

   - ☐ good manners
   - ☑ neatly dressed
   - ☐ pleasant smile
   - ☑ nice personality
   - ☐ congeniality
   - ☑ honesty
   - ☐ affectionate
   - ☐ friendly
   - ☐ sociability

2. How should he be dressed?

   - ☑ dressed up
   - ☐ dressed down
   - ☐ extra casual
   - ☐ does not matter

3. Should he be smiling?

   - ☑ yes
   - ☐ no

4. What style of hair do you like?

   - ☐ long
   - ☐ short
   - ☐ pony tail
   - ☐ bald

   other: all of the above

5. Do you like a man that you just met to be:

   - ☐ serious
   - ☑ comical
   - ☐ romantic

6. What is the first thing a man could say to you that would make you feel good?

   "Hello, how are you — my name is full name

7. What was the nicest, unusual or funniest line a man has ever told you?

"Hi, I've been waiting for you all night."

8. What was the nicest compliment a man has ever paid you?

"You are pretty - not fine - simply pretty"

9. What is the biggest turn off about a man in your opinion?

"Hey Baby - what's your name?"

10. What would be the worst thing a man could say, when he first approaches you?

You sure look sexy!

11. What is the first thing you look at on a man?

- ☐ hair
- ☑ height
- ☐ muscles
- ☐ buns
- ☐ eyes
- ☐ weight
- ☐ other

INTERVIEW FOR WOMEN

THANK YOU FOR TAKING THE TIME TO FILL OUT THIS SURVEY. I AM CURRENTLY DOING RESEARCH FOR A NEW BOOK AND ALL INFORMATION RECEIVED IS ANONYMOUS.

1. What top 3 attributes do you expect men to have when he approaches you.

O good manners	O honesty
O neatly dressed	O affectionate
O pleasant smile	O friendly
O nice personality	O sociability
O congeniality	

2. How should he be dressed?

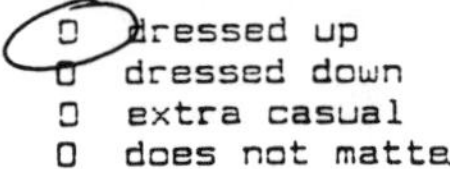

O dressed up
O dressed down
O extra casual
O does not matter

3. Should he be smiling?

O yes
O no

4. What style of hair do you like?

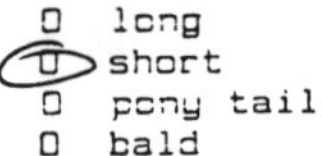

O long
O short
O pony tail
O bald

5. Do you like a man that you just met to be:

O serious
O comical
O romantic

6. What is the first thing a man could say to you that would make you feel good?

Compliment me. on my looks, or what I am wearing.

7. What was the nicest, unusual or funniest line a man has ever told you?

That I aroused him as much as he ever has been by any other woman.

8. What was the nicest compliment a man has ever paid you?

That I was as beautiful inside as I was on the outside.

9. What is the biggest turn off about a man in your opinion?

When he calls me "hey baby" as I am walking

10. What would be the worst thing a man could say, when he first approaches you?

Are you married.

11. What is the first thing you look at on a man?

- ☐ hair
- ☐ height
- ☐ muscles
- ☐ buns
- ☐ eyes
- ☐ weight
- ☑ other

his dress and how he ~~carries~~ conducts himself.

INTERVIEW FOR WOMEN

THANK YOU FOR TAKING THE TIME TO FILL OUT THIS SURVEY. I AM CURRENTLY DOING RESEARCH FOR A NEW BOOK AND ALL INFORMATION RECEIVED IS ANONYMOUS.

1. What top 3 attributes do you expect men to have when he approaches you.

   O good manners
   O neatly dressed
   X pleasant smile
   O nice personality
   O congeniality
   X honesty
   X affectionate
   O friendly
   O sociability

2. How should he be dressed?

   O dressed up
   O dressed down
   O extra casual
   X does not matter as long as it is appropriate for the occasion

3. Should he be smiling?

   X yes
   O no

4. What style of hair do you like?

   O long
   O short
   O pony tail
   O bald
   Doesn't matter as long as its clean.

5. Do you like a man that you just met to be:

   O serious
   X comical
   O romantic

6. What is the first thing a man could say to you that would make you feel good?

   A sincere compliment of; physical appearence
   nice smile.

7. What was the nicest, unusual or funniest line a man has ever told you?

   "Lines" don't work. sincerity does

8. What was the nicest compliment a man has ever paid you?

   You're always smiling

9. What is the biggest turn off about a man in your opinion?

   obnoxious, rudeness.

10. What would be the worst thing a man could say, when he first approaches you?

    "Do you come here often?"

    I honestly don't know I've been married since I was 20. 11½ years.

11. What is the first thing you look at on a man?

O hair	O eyes
O height	X weight
O muscles	O other
O buns	

INTERVIEW FOR WOMEN

THANK YOU FOR TAKING THE TIME TO FILL OUT THIS SURVEY. I AM CURRENTLY DOING RESEARCH FOR A NEW BOOK AND ALL INFORMATION RECEIVED IS ANONYMOUS.

1. What top 3 attributes do you expect men to have when he approaches you.

✓ good manners	O honesty
O neatly dressed	O affectionate
O pleasant smile	✓ friendly
✓ nice personality	O sociability
O congeniality	

2. How should he be dressed?

   ✓ dressed up
   O dressed down
   O extra casual
   O does not matter

3. Should he be smiling?

   ✓ yes (of course he just met me)
   O no

4. What style of hair do you like?

   O long
   ✓ short
   O pony tail
   O bald

5. Do you like a man that you just met to be:

   O serious
   ✓ comical
   O romantic

6. What is the first thing a man could say to you that would make you feel good?

   ~~If he had his ... on him~~ can I buy you a drink.

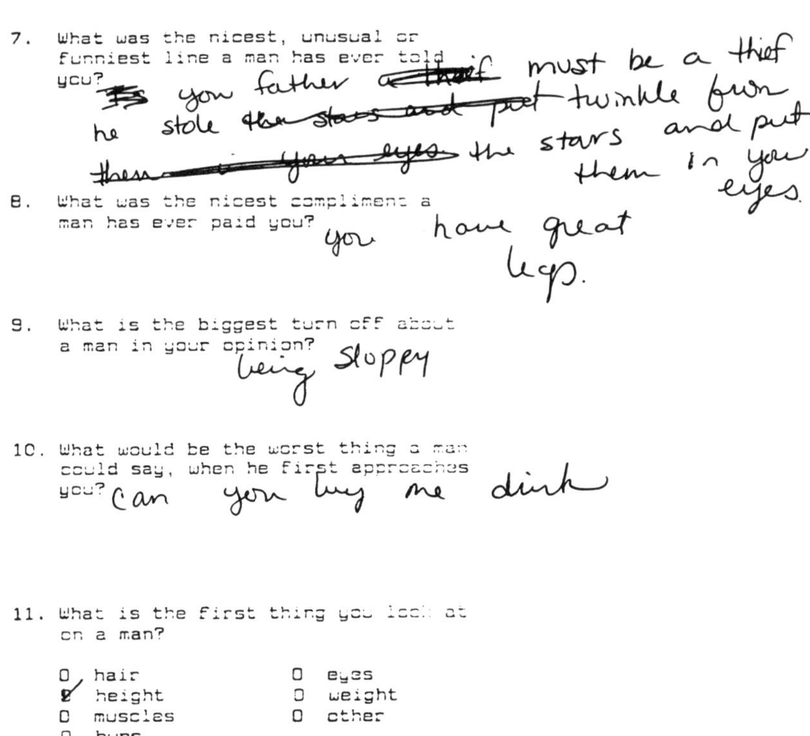

7. What was the nicest, unusual or funniest line a man has ever told you?
you father must be a thief he stole the twinkle from the stars and put them in you eyes.

8. What was the nicest compliment a man has ever paid you?
you have great legs.

9. What is the biggest turn off about a man in your opinion?
being sloppy

10. What would be the worst thing a man could say, when he first approaches you?
Can you buy me drink

11. What is the first thing you look at on a man?

- [ ] hair
- [x] height
- [ ] muscles
- [ ] buns
- [ ] eyes
- [ ] weight
- [ ] other

INTERVIEW FOR WOMEN

THANK YOU FOR TAKING THE TIME TO FILL OUT THIS SURVEY. I AM CURRENTLY DOING RESEARCH FOR A NEW BOOK AND ALL INFORMATION RECEIVED IS ANONYMOUS.

1. What top 3 attributes do you expect men to have when he approaches you.

   - O good manners
   - X neatly dressed
   - O pleasant smile
   - X nice personality
   - O congeniality
   - O honesty
   - O affectionate
   - X friendly
   - O sociability

2. How should he be dressed?

   - X dressed up
   - O dressed down
   - O extra casual
   - O does not matter

3. Should he be smiling?

   - X yes
   - O no

4. What style of hair do you like?

   - O long
   - X short
   - O pony tail
   - O bald

5. Do you like a man that you just met to be:

   - O serious
   - X comical
   - O romantic

6. What is the first thing a man could say to you that would make you feel good?

   When he gives me a compliment.

7. What was the nicest, unusual or funniest line a man has ever told you?

I have Nice eyes

8. What was the nicest compliment a man has ever paid you?

I have nice eyes.

9. What is the biggest turn off about a man in your opinion?

When he is too serious

10. What would be the worst thing a man could say, when he first approaches you?

Have I met you somewhere before.

11. What is the first thing you look at on a man?

- [x] hair
- [x] height
- [x] muscles
- [x] buns
- [x] eyes
- [x] weight
- [ ] other

INTERVIEW FOR WOMEN

THANK YOU FOR TAKING THE TIME TO FILL OUT THIS SURVEY. CURRENTLY DOING RESEARCH FOR A NEW BOOK AND ALL INFORMA RECEIVED IS ANONYMOUS.

1. What top 3 attributes do you expect men to have when he approaches you.

- [x] good manners
- [ ] neatly dressed
- [ ] pleasant smile
- [x] nice personality
- [ ] congeniality
- [ ] honesty
- [ ] affectionate
- [x] friendly
- [ ] sociability

2. How should he be dressed?

- [ ] dressed up
- [ ] dressed down
- [ ] extra casual
- [x] does not matter

3. Should he be smiling?

- [x] yes
- [ ] no

4. What style of hair do you like?

- [ ] long
- [ ] short
- [ ] pony tail
- [ ] bald

it doesn't matter

5. Do you like a man that you just met to be:

- [ ] serious
- [x] comical
- [ ] romantic

6. What is the first thing a man could say to you that would make you feel good?

I have a good sense of humor or if he tells me I'm intelligent

7. What was the nicest, unusual or funniest line a man has ever told you?

Its not really a line but a man sang O Danny Boy to win my heart (and he did)

8. What was the nicest compliment a man has ever paid you?

I knew the first time I saw you I was in love with you

9. What is the biggest turn off about a man in your opinion?

A man w/out a sense of humor
A man w/ a one track mind
An ignorant man - in every sense of the word

10. What is the worst thing a man has ever said to you?

"Hey, nice tits"

11. What is the first thing you look on a man?

- [ ] hair
- [ ] height
- [ ] muscles
- [ ] buns
- [x] eyes
- [ ] weight
- [x] other

teeth

INTERVIEW FOR WOMEN

THANK YOU FOR TAKING THE TIME TO FILL OUT THIS SURVEY. I AM CURRENTLY DOING RESEARCH FOR A NEW BOOK AND ALL INFORMATION RECEIVED IS ANONYMOUS.

1. What top 3 attributes do you expect men to have when he approaches you.

O good manners
O neatly dressed
O pleasant smile
O nice personality
O congeniality
O honesty
O affectionate
O friendly
O sociability

2. How should he be dressed?

O dressed up
O dressed down
O extra casual
O does not matter

3. Should he be smiling?

O yes
O no

4. What style of hair do you like?

O long
O short
O pony tail
O bald

5. Do you like a man that you just met to be:

O serious
O comical
O romantic

6. What is the first thing a man could say to you that would make you feel good?

You're thighs look great!

7. What was the nicest, unusual or funniest line a man has ever told you? "Well, I'd buy you a drink, but I see you already have one - I'd ask you to dance - but I don't like to dance so - I guess I'll just strike up a conversation."

8. What was the nicest compliment a man has ever paid you?
This is the most fun I've ever had.

9. What is the biggest turn off about a man in your opinion?
when they act like a jerk - like Mr. Macho.

10. What is the worst thing a man has ever said to you?
Come on - it's late - let me buy you a drink

11. What is the first thing you look on a man?

O hair	O eyes
(O) height	O weight
O muscles	O other
O buns	

Dont be afraid to go over to a group of girls!!

INTERVIEW FOR WOMEN

THANK YOU FOR TAKING THE TIME TO FILL OUT THIS SURVEY. CURRENTLY DOING RESEARCH FOR A NEW BOOK AND ALL INFORMA RECEIVED IS ANONYMOUS.

1. What top 3 attributes do you expect men to have when he approaches you.

- ☒ good manners
- ☐ neatly dressed
- ☐ pleasant smile
- ☒ nice personality
- ☒ congeniality
- ☐ honesty
- ☐ affectionate
- ☐ friendly
- ☐ sociability

2. How should he be dressed?

- ☐ dressed up
- ☐ dressed down
- ☒ extra casual
- ☐ does not matter

3. Should he be smiling?

- ☒ yes
- ☐ no

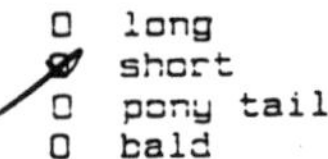

4. What style of hair do you like?

- ☐ long
- ☒ short
- ☐ pony tail
- ☐ bald

5. Do you like a man that you just met to be:

- ☐ serious
- ☒ comical
- ☐ romantic

6. What is the first thing a man could say to you that would make you feel good?

I think your a nice girl, and I hope maybe we could get together sometime.

7. What was the nicest, unusual or funniest line a man has ever told you? I think me + you would be perfect together, Lets get married!?

8. What was the nicest compliment a man has ever paid you? you are buetiful

9. What is the biggest turn off about a man in your opinion? Dirty mouth. No manners!

10. What is the worst thing a man has ever said to you? If he doesn't like my appearance!

11. What is the first thing you look on a man?

- ☐ hair
- ☐ height
- ☐ muscles
- ☐ buns
- ☒ eyes
- ☐ weight
- ☐ other

INTERVIEW FOR WOMEN

THANK YOU FOR TAKING THE TIME TO FILL OUT THIS SURVEY. I AM CURRENTLY DOING RESEARCH FOR A NEW BOOK AND ALL INFORMATION RECEIVED IS ANONYMOUS.

1. What top 3 attributes do you expect men to have when he approaches you.

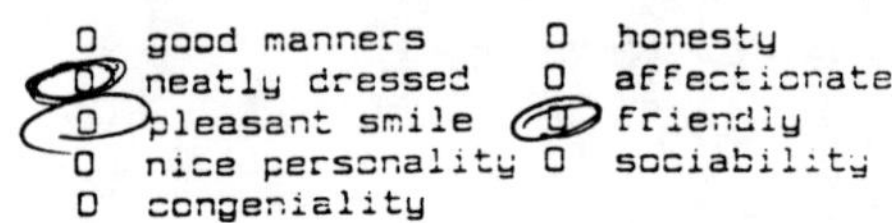

O good manners
O neatly dressed
O pleasant smile
O nice personality
O congeniality
O honesty
O affectionate
O friendly
O sociability

2. How should he be dressed?

O dressed up
O dressed down
O extra casual
O does not matter

3. Should he be smiling?

O yes
O no

4. What style of hair do you like?

O long
O short
O pony tail
O bald

5. Do you like a man that you just met to be:

O serious
O comical
O romantic

6. What is the first thing a man could say to you that would make you feel good? A Simple Hello not an old Stupid line.

7. What was the nicest, unusual or funniest line a man has ever told you? He told me I look very Romantic.

8. What was the nicest compliment a man has ever paid you? That I am very pretty and not stuck up. great personality.

9. What is the biggest turn off about a man in your opinion? when they think there better then every one else. Gods Gift to Women

10. What would be the worst thing a man could say, when he first approaches you? I would like to go to Bed with you. (Has Happen)

11. What is the first thing you look at on a man?

- O hair
- O height
- O muscles
- O buns
- O eyes
- O weight
- X other everthing

INTERVIEW FOR WOMEN

THANK YOU FOR TAKING THE TIME TO FILL OUT THIS SURVEY. I AM CURRENTLY DOING RESEARCH FOR A NEW BOOK AND ALL INFORMATION RECEIVED IS ANONYMOUS.

1. What top 3 attributes do you expect men to have when he approaches you.

   O good manners
   O neatly dressed
   O pleasant smile
   O nice personality
   O congeniality
   O honesty
   O affectionate
   O friendly
   O sociability

2. How should he be dressed?

   O dressed up
   O dressed down
   O extra casual
   O does not matter

3. Should he be smiling?

   O yes
   O no

4. What style of hair do you like?

   O long
   O short
   O pony tail
   O bald

5. Do you like a man that you just met to be:

   O serious
   O comical
   O romantic

6. What is the first thing a man could say to you that would make you feel good?

   A sincere compliment

7. What was the nicest, unusual or funniest line a man has ever told you?

That I looked like the person that ~~they~~ he had always dreamed of marrying + spending the rest of ~~this~~ life ~~together~~ with.

8. What was the nicest compliment a man has ever paid you?

~~Looks &~~ nice eyes - Look very good ~~today~~ (Sincere)

9. What is the biggest turn off about a man in your opinion?

trying to impress

10. What would be the worst thing a man could say, when he first approaches you?

~~[illegible]~~ Hey baby what are you doing Later (said w/ expectations)

11. What is the first thing you look at on a man?

- ☐ hair
- ☐ height
- ☐ muscles
- ☐ buns
- ☑ eyes
- ☐ weight
- ☐ other

INTERVIEW FOR WOMEN

THANK YOU FOR TAKING THE TIME TO FILL OUT THIS SURVEY. I AM CURRENTLY DOING RESEARCH FOR A NEW BOOK AND ALL INFORMATION RECEIVED IS ANONYMOUS.

1. What top 3 attributes do you expect men to have when he approaches you.

- [x] good manners
- [ ] neatly dressed
- [ ] pleasant smile
- [ ] nice personality
- [ ] congeniality
- [ ] honesty
- [ ] affectionate
- [x] friendly
- [x] sociability

2. How should he be dressed?

- [ ] dressed up
- [ ] dressed down
- [ ] extra casual
- [x] does not matter

3. Should he be smiling?

- [x] yes
- [ ] no

4. What style of hair do you like?

- [ ] long
- [ ] short
- [x] pony tail
- [ ] bald

5. Do you like a man that you just met to be:

- [ ] serious
- [x] comical
- [ ] romantic

6. What is the first thing a man could say to you that would make you feel good?

Any kind of compliment on my certain tastes or styles. (Something smart or sweet, not sexual.)

7. What was the nicest, unusual or funniest line a man has ever told you? The nicest thing ever said was, "All the years I've known you, I've had such a crush on you, but never told you 'cause I figured you wouldn't give me a chance." P.S. (+ I would have.)

8. What was the nicest compliment a man has ever paid you?
"You have a great voice." or "I love your hair."

9. What is the biggest turn off about a man in your opinion?
Bad hygiene

10. What would be the worst thing a man could say, when he first approaches you?
"Let's get a six-pack + go back to my place." (Yuck!)

11. What is the first thing you look at on a man?

- ☑ hair
- ☑ height
- ☐ muscles
- ☐ buns
- ☐ eyes
- ☐ weight
- ☐ other

INTERVIEW FOR WOMEN

THANK YOU FOR TAKING THE TIME TO FILL OUT THIS SURVEY. I AM CURRENTLY DOING RESEARCH FOR A NEW BOOK AND ALL INFORMATION RECEIVED IS ANONYMOUS.

1. What top 3 attributes do you expect men to have when he approaches you.

   - X good manners
   - O neatly dressed
   - O pleasant smile
   - O nice personality
   - O congeniality
   - O honesty
   - O affectionate
   - X friendly
   - X sociability

2. How should he be dressed?

   - O dressed up
   - O dressed down
   - O extra casual
   - X does not matter

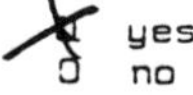

3. Should he be smiling?

   - X yes
   - O no

4. What style of hair do you like?

   - O long
   - O short
   - X pony tail
   - O bald

5. Do you like a man that you just met to be:

   - O serious
   - X comical
   - O romantic

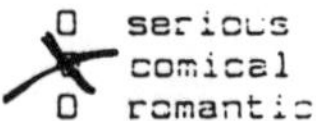

6. What is the first thing a man could say to you that would make you feel good?

   To be complemented in a nice + respected way.

7. What was the nicest, unusual or funniest line a man has ever told you?

   Before he approaches me he Saids I asked your dad if I could date you.

8. What was the nicest compliment a man has ever paid you?

   Nice Legs + a wonderful Smile!

9. What is the biggest turn off about a man in your opinion?

   BAD hygiene

10. What would be the worst thing a man could say, when he first approaches you?

    "Lets get a bottle of Wine and go back to my place or yours"

11. What is the first thing you look at on a man?

X hair	X eyes
O height	X weight
O muscles	O other
O buns	

INTERVIEW FOR WOMEN

THANK YOU FOR TAKING THE TIME TO FILL OUT THIS SURVEY. I AM CURRENTLY DOING RESEARCH FOR A NEW BOOK AND ALL INFORMATION RECEIVED IS ANONYMOUS.

1. What top 3 attributes do you expect men to have when he approaches you.

   ✓ good manners
   O neatly dressed
   O pleasant smile
   ✓ nice personality
   O congeniality
   O honesty
   O affectionate
   ✓ friendly
   O sociability

2. How should he be dressed?

   O dressed up
   O dressed down
   O extra casual
   ✓ does not matter

3. Should he be smiling?

   ✓ yes
   O no

4. What style of hair do you like?

   O long
   ✓ short
   O pony tail
   O bald

5. Do you like a man that you just met to be:

   O serious
   ✓ comical
   O romantic

6. What is the first thing a man could say to you that would make you feel good?

   You have such a nice smile.

7. What was the nicest, unusual or funniest line a man has ever told you?

I respect you too much to talk badly (cuss) in front of you

8. What was the nicest compliment a man has ever paid you?

That smile is devastating

9. What is the biggest turn off about a man in your opinion?

Dirty clothes, needs a shower

10. What would be the worst thing a man could say, when he first approaches you?

Call me babe or sweetheart when I don't know him.

11. What is the first thing you look at on a man?

O hair	✓ eyes
O height	O weight
O muscles	O other
O buns	

INTERVIEW FOR WOMEN

THANK YOU FOR TAKING THE TIME TO FILL OUT THIS SURVEY. I AM CURRENTLY DOING RESEARCH FOR A NEW BOOK AND ALL INFORMATION RECEIVED IS ANONYMOUS.

1. What top 3 attributes do you expect men to have when he approaches you.

☑	good manners	☑	honesty
O	neatly dressed	O	affectionate
O	pleasant smile	O	friendly
O	nice personality	☑	sociability
O	congeniality		

2. How should he be dressed?

   - O dressed up
   - O dressed down
   - O extra casual
   - ☑ does not matter

3. Should he be smiling?

   - ☑ yes
   - O no

4. What style of hair do you like?

   - O long
   - O short
   - O pony tail
   - O bald

   All of the above

5. Do you like a man that you just met to be:

   - O serious
   - ☑ comical
   - O romantic

6. What is the first thing a man could say to you that would make you feel good? About. my dress & figure

7. What was the nicest, unusual or funniest line a man has ever told you? "Gee, you look like Heather Locklear

8. What was the nicest compliment a man has ever paid you? About my eyes

9. What is the biggest turn off about a man in your opinion? Being Drunk & obnoctious

10. What would be the worst thing a man could say, when he first approaches you? Ask for oral sex

11. What is the first thing you look at on a man?

- ☐ hair
- ☐ height
- ☐ muscles
- ☐ buns
- ☐ eyes
- ☐ weight
- ☑ other

INTERVIEW FOR WOMEN

THANK YOU FOR TAKING THE TIME TO FILL OUT THIS SURVEY. I AM CURRENTLY DOING RESEARCH FOR A NEW BOOK AND ALL INFORMATION RECEIVED IS ANONYMOUS.

1. What top 3 attributes do you expect men to have when he approaches you.

   - ✓ good manners
   - ✓ neatly dressed
   - O pleasant smile
   - ✓ nice personality
   - O congeniality
   - O honesty
   - O affectionate
   - O friendly
   - O sociability

2. How should he be dressed?

   - ✓ dressed up
   - O dressed down
   - O extra casual
   - O does not matter

3. Should he be smiling?

   - ✓ yes
   - O no

4. What style of hair do you like?

   - O long
   - ✓ short
   - O pony tail
   - O bald

5. Do you like a man that you just met to be:

   - O serious
   - O comical
   - ✓ romantic

6. What is the first thing a man could say to you that would make you feel good?

   TELL ME how much he admires ME.

7. What was the nicest, unusual or funniest line a man has ever told you?

Nicest - you have a beautiful Smile

8. What was the nicest compliment a man has ever paid you?

Said I reminded him of Lola Falana

9. What is the biggest turn off about a man in your opinion?

ONE That has a body odor & ONE that Swears

10. What would be the worst thing a man could say, when he first approaches you?

SEX

11. What is the first thing you look at on a man?

- O hair
- O height
- O muscles
- O buns
- ✓ eyes
- O weight
- ✓ other Shoulders

INTERVIEW FOR WOMEN

THANK YOU FOR TAKING THE TIME TO FILL OUT THIS SURVEY. I AM CURRENTLY DOING RESEARCH FOR A NEW BOOK AND ALL INFORMATION RECEIVED IS ANONYMOUS.

1. What top 3 attributes do you expect men to have when he approaches you.

- [x] good manners
- [ ] neatly dressed
- [ ] pleasant smile
- [x] nice personality
- [ ] congeniality
- [ ] honesty
- [ ] affectionate
- [x] friendly
- [ ] sociability

2. How should he be dressed?

- [ ] dressed up
- [ ] dressed down
- [ ] extra casual
- [x] does not matter

3. Should he be smiling?

- [x] yes
- [ ] no

4. What style of hair do you like?

- [x] long
- [ ] short
- [ ] pony tail
- [ ] bald

5. Do you like a man that you just met to be:

- [ ] serious
- [x] comical
- [ ] romantic

6. What is the first thing a man could say to you that would make you feel good?

I really wanted to meet you

7. What was the nicest, unusual or funniest line a man has ever told you? Thin tall guy bumped into me & said "Excuse me my massive body always gets in the way"

8. What was the nicest compliment a man has ever paid you? That I'm nice

9. What is the biggest turn off about a man in your opinion? Crude, drunk men Smoking, bad teeth

10. What would be the worst thing a man could say, when he first approaches you? You turn me on or something like that

11. What is the first thing you look at on a man?

- ☒ hair
- ☐ height
- ☐ muscles
- ☐ buns
- ☐ eyes
- ☒ weight
- ☐ other

INTERVIEW FOR WOMEN

THANK YOU FOR TAKING THE TIME TO FILL OUT THIS SURVEY. I AM CURRENTLY DOING RESEARCH FOR A NEW BOOK AND ALL INFORMATION RECEIVED IS ANONYMOUS.

1. What top 3 attributes do you expect men to have when he approaches you.

   - X good manners
   - 0 neatly dressed
   - 0 pleasant smile
   - X nice personality
   - 0 congeniality
   - 0 honesty
   - 0 affectionate
   - X friendly
   - 0 sociability

2. How should he be dressed?

   - 0 dressed up
   - X dressed down
   - 0 extra casual
   - 0 does not matter

3. Should he be smiling?

   - X yes
   - 0 no

4. What style of hair do you like?

   - 0 long
   - X short
   - 0 pony tail
   - 0 bald

5. Do you like a man that you just met to be:

   - 0 serious
   - X comical
   - 0 romantic

6. What is the first thing a man could say to you that would make you feel good?

   complement you on your dress/attire

7. What was the nicest, unusual or funniest line a man has ever told you?

what's your favorite ice cream

8. What was the nicest compliment a man has ever paid you?

eyes

9. What is the biggest turn off about a man in your opinion?

too pushy / BO

10. What would be the worst thing a man could say, when he first approaches you?

if he makes sexist comments.

11. What is the first thing you look at on a man?

- ☐ hair
- ☐ height
- ☐ muscles
- ☐ buns
- ☒ eyes
- ☐ weight
- ☐ other

INTERVIEW FOR WOMEN

THANK YOU FOR TAKING THE TIME TO FILL OUT THIS SURVEY. I AM CURRENTLY DOING RESEARCH FOR A NEW BOOK AND ALL INFORMATION RECEIVED IS ANONYMOUS.

1. What top 3 attributes do you expect men to have when he approaches you.

- ☑ good manners
- ☐ neatly dressed
- ☑ pleasant smile
- ☑ nice personality
- ☐ congeniality
- ☑ honesty
- ☐ affectionate
- ☐ friendly
- ☐ sociability

2. How should he be dressed?

- ☐ dressed up
- ☐ dressed down
- ☐ extra casual
- ☑ does not matter

3. Should he be smiling?

- ☑ yes
- ☐ no

4. What style of hair do you like?

- ☐ long
- ☑ short
- ☐ pony tail
- ☐ bald

5. Do you like a man that you just met to be:

- ☐ serious
- ☑ comical
- ☐ romantic

tough one

6. What is the first thing a man could say to you that would make you feel good?

How could someone so beautiful be so intelligent

7. What was the nicest, unusual or funniest line a man has ever told you?

She's a good cook ... when she cooks!

8. What was the nicest compliment a man has ever paid you?

You're not only beautiful, but you're intelligent.

9. What is the biggest turn off about a man in your opinion?

chauvinism

10. What would be the worst thing a man could say, when he first approaches you?

Hey babe

11. What is the first thing you look at on a man?

- ☐ hair
- ☐ height
- ☐ muscles
- ☐ buns
- ☑ eyes
- ☐ weight
- ☐ other

INTERVIEW FOR WOMEN

THANK YOU FOR TAKING THE TIME TO FILL OUT THIS SURVEY. I AM CURRENTLY DOING RESEARCH FOR A NEW BOOK AND ALL INFORMATION RECEIVED IS ANONYMOUS.

1. What top 3 attributes do you expect men to have when he approaches you.

   - [ ] good manners
   - [ ] neatly dressed
   - [x] pleasant smile
   - [x] nice personality
   - [ ] congeniality
   - [ ] honesty
   - [ ] affectionate
   - [x] friendly
   - [ ] sociability

2. How should he be dressed?

   - [ ] dressed up
   - [x] dressed down
   - [ ] extra casual
   - [ ] does not matter

3. Should he be smiling?

   - [x] yes
   - [ ] no

4. What style of hair do you like?

   - [ ] long
   - [x] short
   - [ ] pony tail
   - [ ] bald

5. Do you like a man that you just met to be:

   - [ ] serious
   - [x] comical
   - [ ] romantic

6. What is the first thing a man could say to you that would make you feel good?

   You have a great Personality.

7. What was the nicest, unusual or funniest line a man has ever told you?

My last name is Italian.... but I'm 1/2 Irish!

8. What was the nicest compliment a man has ever paid you?

you're such a down to earth girl + beautiful too!

9. What is the biggest turn off about a man in your opinion?

When he's impressed with himself.

10. What would be the worst thing a man could say, when he first approaches you?

"Come here often?"

11. What is the first thing you look at on a man?

- ☐ hair
- ☐ height
- ☐ muscles
- ☐ buns
- ☐ eyes
- ☐ weight
- ☒ other → Smile

INTERVIEW FOR WOMEN

THANK YOU FOR TAKING THE TIME TO FILL OUT THIS SURVEY. I AM CURRENTLY DOING RESEARCH FOR A NEW BOOK AND ALL INFORMATION RECEIVED IS ANONYMOUS.

1. What top 3 attributes do you expect men to have when he approaches you.

   - ✓ good manners
   - O neatly dressed
   - O pleasant smile
   - O nice personality
   - O congeniality
   - O honesty
   - O affectionate
   - O friendly
   - O sociability

2. How should he be dressed?

   - O dressed up
   - O dressed down
   - O extra casual
   - ✓ does not matter *as long as neat and clean*

3. Should he be smiling?

   - ✓ yes
   - O no

4. What style of hair do you like?

   - O long
   - ✓ short
   - O pony tail
   - O bald

5. Do you like a man that you just met to be:

   - ✓ serious
   - O comical
   - O romantic

6. What is the first thing a man could say to you that would make you feel good?

   I look young & beautiful.

7. What was the nicest, unusual or funniest line a man has ever told you?

I am warm and loving.

8. What was the nicest compliment a man has ever paid you?

I am ~~warm and giving and~~ the best thing that ever happened to him.

9. What is the biggest turn off about a man in your opinion?

Sloppy Eating

10. What would be the worst thing a man could say, when he first approaches you?

I am unattractive.

11. What is the first thing you look at on a man?

- O hair
- O height
- O muscles
- O buns
- ☑ eyes
- O weight
- O other

INTERVIEW FOR WOMEN

THANK YOU FOR TAKING THE TIME TO FILL OUT THIS SURVEY. I AM CURRENTLY DOING RESEARCH FOR A NEW BOOK AND ALL INFORMATION RECEIVED IS ANONYMOUS.

1. What top 3 attributes do you expect men to have when he approaches you.

X good manners
O neatly dressed
O pleasant smile
X nice personality
O congeniality
X honesty
O affectionate
O friendly
O sociability

2. How should he be dressed?

O dressed up
O dressed down
O extra casual
X does not matter

3. Should he be smiling?

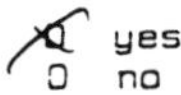
X yes
O no

4. What style of hair do you like?

O long
X short
O pony tail
O bald

5. Do you like a man that you just met to be:

X serious
O comical
O romantic

6. What is the first thing a man could say to you that would make you feel good?

Compliment me sincerely.

7. What was the nicest, unusual or funniest line a man has ever told you?

will you marry me?!

8. What was the nicest compliment a man has ever paid you?

What a beautiful person you are!

9. What is the biggest turn off about a man in your opinion?

not liking what you have on.

10. What would be the worst thing a man could say, when he first approaches you?

burping or talking loud.

11. What is the first thing you look at on a man?

- ☐ hair
- ☐ height
- ☐ muscles
- ☐ buns
- ☒ eyes & smile!
- ☐ weight
- ☐ other

I hope you read each one of the interviews. It's important to get a feel for what these women want by reading them for yourself.

Now I would like to analyze each question individually. What I did was tally all the answers from the over two thousand interviews to give you, among other things, what the top answers were.

QUESTION #1: WHAT TOP 3 ATTRIBUTES DO YOU EXPECT A MAN TO HAVE WHEN HE APPROACHES YOU?

If you look at GRAPH I, you will see that the top attribute a man must have when approaching a woman is a "nice personality." "Nice personality" was the number one answer given by these beautiful women. This means, excluding everything else for a moment, a beautiful woman wants to be treated delicately. In a pleasing and agreeable way. They want a respectable and virtuous type of man to approach them. One who has a nice personality excludes anything that is offensive or unpleasant. One with charm and is pleasing to talk with.

"Good manners" was the second top answer given in the interviews. Beautiful women expect us to be well mannered. That means we must behave in a sociably acceptable way. We must be in control of ourselves at all times with this beautiful lady. We must be well mannered in the specified way outlined by society. No belching, burping, cursing, farting - well you get the picture.

The number three top answer for this question was "honesty." The woman of today doesn't want to hear lies anymore. They are sick of it. They are too smart for that.

They know right away when we lie to them. Don't try to deceive them, it is just no good. It's better to be truthful now-a-days. It shows you have integrity. Women admire that. You appear genuine and real to the woman you are talking to. I can't tell you how many times women have told me that the guy they were talking to was "so full of shit." Everybody's rich or the president of I.B.M. Those lines just don't make it anymore. You look honorable to a woman when you are honest.

Let's face it, you wouldn't want to be "bullshitted" by someone else. You know when someone is "bullshitting" you. So why try doing it to someone you really want. They will be impressed a million times more by your upright, conscientious behavior than anything else.

"Friendly" was fourth and very close to "honesty." A woman expects a man to respect her for what she is. One should not be hostile in any way, shape, or form. She wants you to be supportive and favor her. Talk about things that interest her. Not what interest you. Find out what her point of view is on certain subjects and see things from that side. Don't criticize anything she is talking about or try to judge her beliefs. Women love to talk about themselves, so be a good listener, no matter how boring it may be. Don't start talking to her about yourself and all the details about your life. You'll lose her interest right away.

Most of the women I talk to in the nightclubs are just dying to tell me what they did all week. Where they went shopping. What store in the mall they bought their clothes. What happened at work. What kind of car they drive or would like to buy. I have never seen a woman happier than when she was talking about herself, especially to someone who looks genuinely interested.

You can make more friends out of these beautiful women, by listening to them and what they have to say

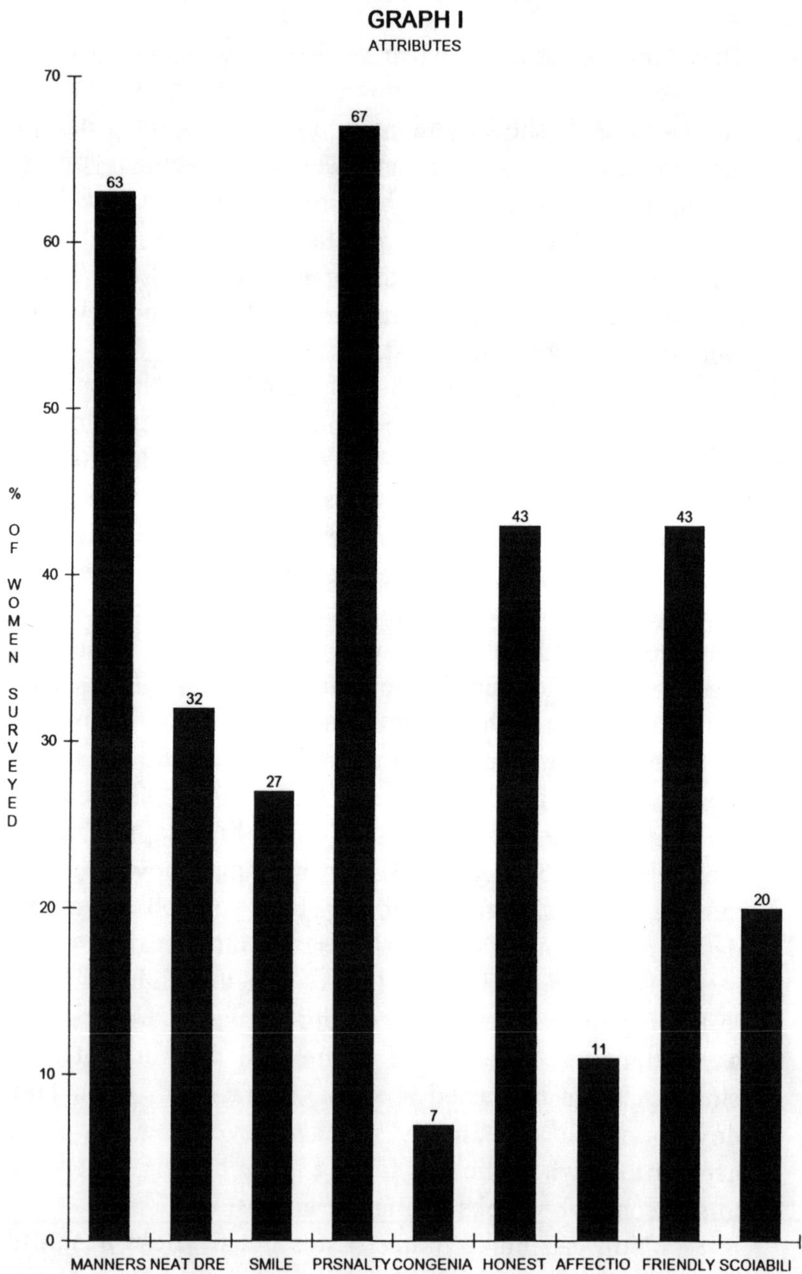
GRAPH I
ATTRIBUTES
% OF WOMEN SURVEYED
70
60
50
40
30
20
10
0
63
32
27
67
7
43
11
43
20
MANNERS
NEAT DRE
SMILE
PRSNALTY
CONGENIA
HONEST
AFFECTIO
FRIENDLY
SCOIABILI

about themselves in ten minutes, than trying to get them to like you by talking about yourself for ten years.

The fifth most popular answer was "neatly dressed." This just means to be dressed orderly, not clothes that are disarranged or sloppy. Simple and tasteful, not all mixed up colors with stripes and plaids going in all different directions. Just clean and neat, as simple as that.

"Pleasant smile" was number six. It gives the impression that you are a warm person inside. It puts people at ease when they see a smile. It makes them feel good. I will elaborate on that later in this chapter.

"Sociability" was the number seven answer in the survey. This means your ability to be gracious, cordial, or affable. It is how pleasant your companionship is with other people. It also has to do with your interaction with a group of people or the members in general.

It pertains to how you participate in a social gathering. Your "sociability" is how well you relate to other people in a given circumstance.

Number eight, and next to the last for question number one, was "affectionate." Beautiful women are not that interested in affection when you first approach them. Later on in a relationship they crave it. But when you first approach them, forget about being mushy or showing any tender affections you may be feeling. They are not interested in it at this point.

QUESTION #2: HOW SHOULD HE BE DRESSED?

The second question in the interview pertained to how one should be dressed. According to the four categories, the number one answer was the fourth choice,

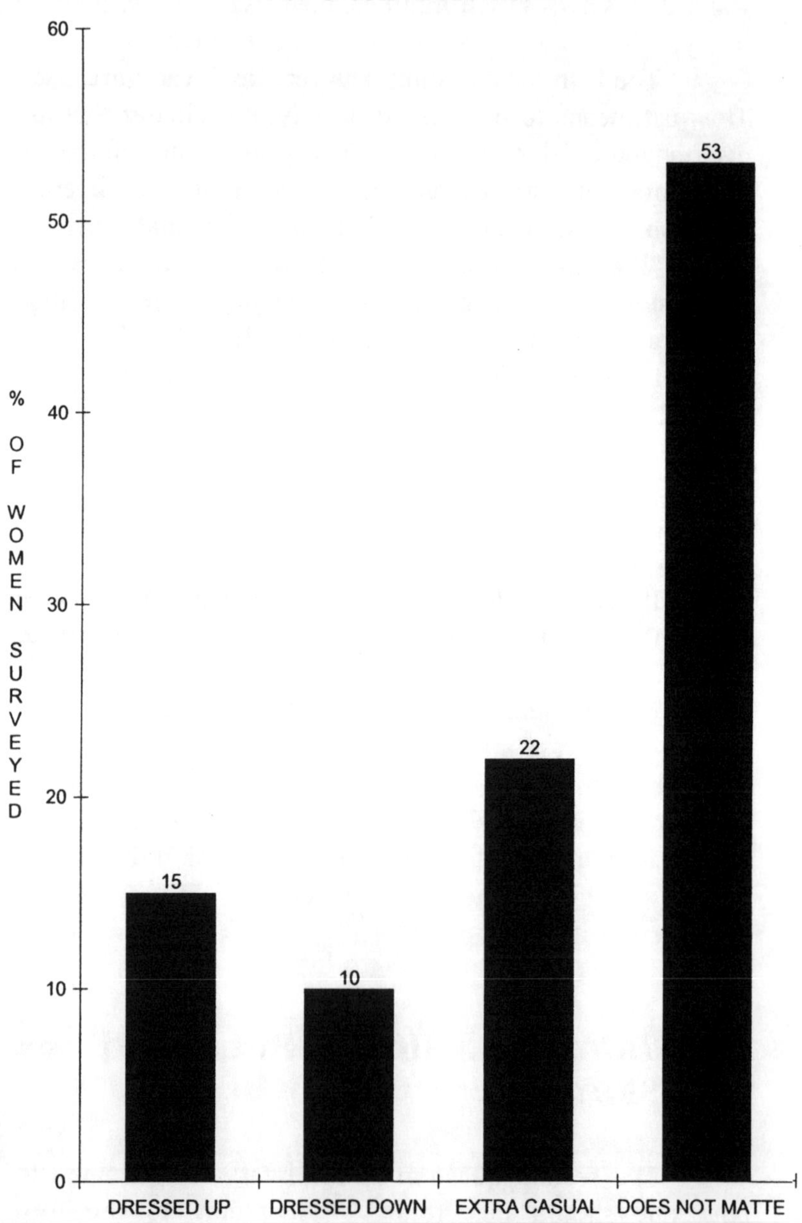
GRAPH II
HOW SHOULD HE BE DRESSED
% OF WOMEN SURVEYED
60
50
40
30
20
10
0
15
10
22
53
DRESSED UP
DRESSED DOWN
EXTRA CASUAL
DOES NOT MATTE

"does not matter," which is good because it takes the pressure off of us. They are not expecting us to be fashion experts. But they do expect us to be clean and neat. This is important to most beautiful women. As I interviewed them, most made a point to say that it did not matter as long as the guy was "not bummy looking." Of the two thousand interviews, a big percent made an extra note next to the category "does not matter" by stating the above.

A quick look at GRAPH II will help you understand, on a percent basis, how they feel about the way we are dressed.

The second most popular answer was "extra casual." A lot of beautiful women crossed out the "extra" in the "extra casual" category, leaving it to read simply "casual." Many women put a note by "casual" stating, "as long as it fits the occasion." So, again, there is not much pressure on the way we are dressed, as long as it fits the occasion.

We can get away with jeans and shirt and even sneakers. Although some clubs won't let you in with sneakers. A lot of places have their own dress code which you will have to abide by if you want to get in.

Third in this category was "dressed up." A small percent of beautiful women expect to be approached by a guy in a suit and tie or even wearing a tux.

Fourth, and final, in this category was "dressed down." This means one with dress pants and shirt, sport jacket, and no tie.

QUESTION #3: SHOULD HE BE SMILING?

A quick look at GRAPH III is all you need to realize how important a smile can be to a beautiful woman. A sincere smile is captivating. It can't be mechanical, it must come from inside. It must be heartwarming. A big percent of the women I interviewed made a point to say that the smile should not be forced. It should not be covering the true self and it should not be pasted on. It must be a natural smile, otherwise, you are not going to fool anyone. Just looking at a beautiful woman makes me want to smile. Just think of all the fun you'll be having with this beautiful woman. That alone is enough to bring out a sincere smile in any man.

I always have a big smile on when a beautiful woman comes into the club. Countless women have told me that my smile made them feel there was someone caring in an atmosphere that seemed harsh, and a bit scary, at times.

If you have a sincere smile on your face when you approach a beautiful woman, you appear more human. Think only happy thoughts on the night you are going out. By controlling your thoughts, you will control your state of mind. Put all your worries aside for the time being. Happiness depends on your inner condition. Practice smiling and positive thoughts before you go out, and keep that state of mind throughout the night. Keep a good mental attitude.

You will brighten the lives of the women you approach with a smile. You are sending a message of good will to her when you smile. Show these beautiful women that there is joy in the world, and you are willing to share it with them. It doesn't cost you a thing to smile, but it enriches the one who receives it. Believe me, these beautiful women have such a huge need for such a simple, yet powerful, gesture as a smile.

The most important thing you get out of the techniques in this book is to do them in a sincere, down to earth, and real way.

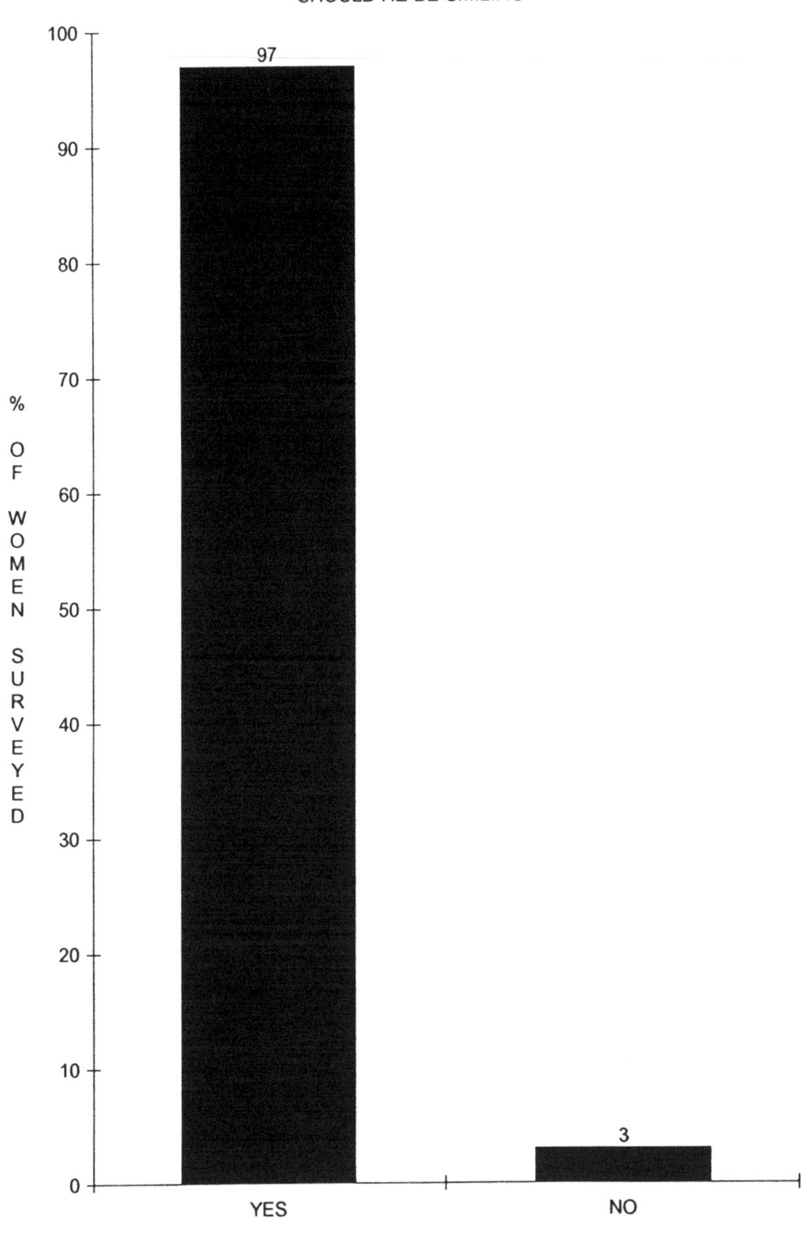
GRAPH III
SHOULD HE BE SMILING
100
90
80
70
60
50
40
30
20
10
0
% OF WOMEN SURVEYED
97
3
YES
NO

QUESTION #4: WHAT STYLE OF HAIR DO YOU LIKE?

I have some surprising facts to give you on this question in the interviews about hair. The number one answer for "style of hair" was "short hair." Look at GRAPH IV for a quick understanding of how beautiful women prefer guys to look. In this day and age, when one would think almost anything goes in hair styles, most beautiful women picked "short hair." They felt that hair was an excellent indicator of how well we groom ourselves and how clean we are. An overwhelming majority picked short hair. They seem to like that neat and orderly look.

The second top answer, but not even close to the number one answer, was "long hair." I know a lot of guys have long hair now-a-days and there is a certain percentage of beautiful women who prefer long hair. If you think you look good with long hair, then keep it. But if you boil this down to a science, short hair is the way to go in your pursuit of beautiful women.

As I conducted the interviews, I told these beautiful women that if they could think of a better answer than the ones on the survey, then please add it in. The third most popular answer was a write-in called "doesn't matter." These women felt it did not matter how a man wore his hair. It was a small percent, as you can see on GRAPH IV, but still it beat out two other categories. They stated that it did not matter how the men wore their hair, as long as it was clean and groomed. That particular comment was prevalent with all the categories under hair.

This next category was a big surprise to me. Having a "ponytail" was fourth as a matter of preference. I thought ponytails were the "in" look today. But it sure was very low on the scale. Ponytails don't seem to impress

GRAPH IV
STYLE OF HAIR
% OF WOMEN SURVEYED
70
60
50
40
30
20
10
0
65
18
4.4
0.6
12
LONG
SHORT
PONYTAIL
BALD
DOES NOT MA

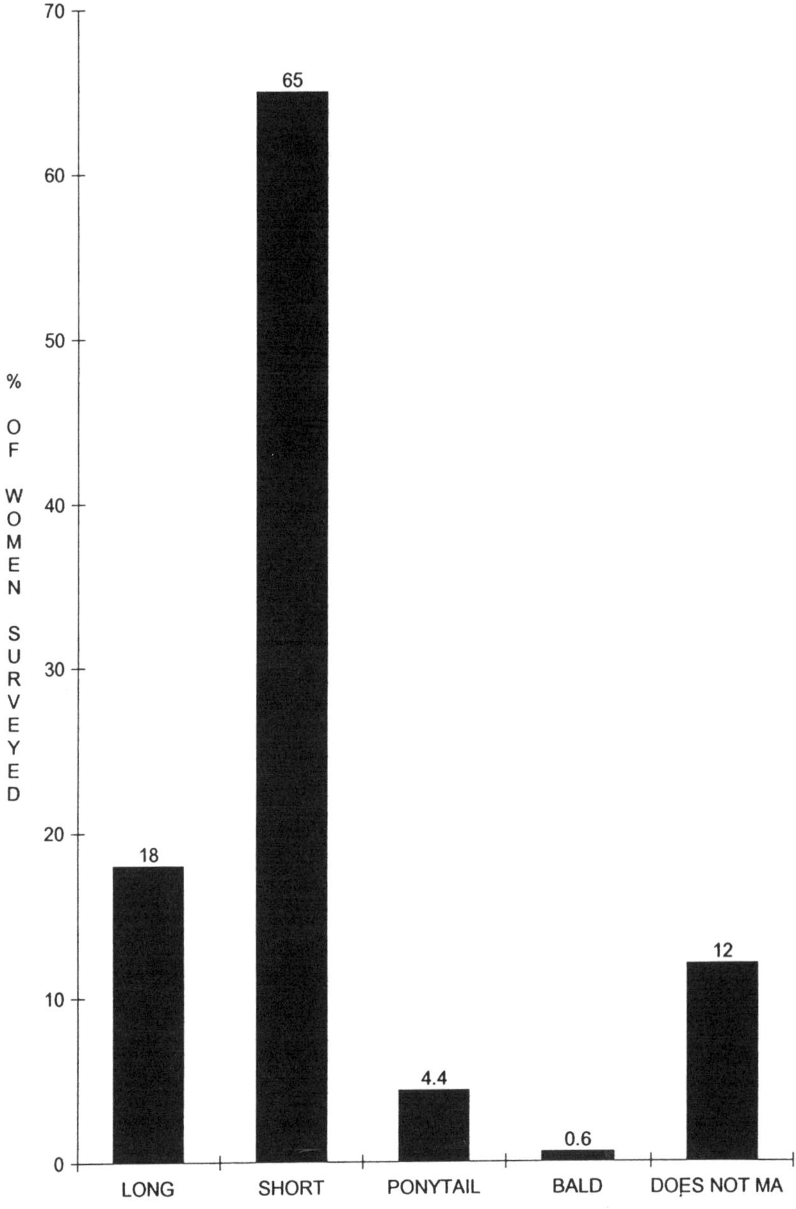

these women. Maybe it is a macho thing among guys. Maybe it will come to its own some day. Perhaps in a few years or so we will get used to looking at it, and it will be accepted by beautiful women. But for now, I have to go with just the facts that only 4% of the women interviewed preferred ponytails.

Last on the list was women who preferred men who were "bald." Point six percent said they liked bald men. This goes against what we have been seeing on television recently. It is supposed to be "in" to shave your head now-a-days. I don't know who this is "in" with. But if you are bald, don't despair. I know a lot of bald guys who followed my techniques and had no problem getting the women they wanted.

QUESTION #5: DO YOU LIKE A MAN THAT YOU JUST MET TO BE SERIOUS, COMICAL, OR ROMANTIC?

The number one answer, and the overwhelming majority, picked "comical." Look at GRAPH V for the percentages. As I interviewed these beautiful women, they stated that they did not want a stand-up comic, nor did they want the guy to tell them jokes. They especially stressed the fact that they didn't want to hear long jokes. By comical they felt one with a sense of humor would suffice.

Some short bit of humor you might throw in during the course of your conversation. If you are not fast witted, try to remember something that struck you as funny and incorporate it into the main stream of your conversation.

For example, if the subject of clothes comes up, you might say, "There was a time when I thought the height of

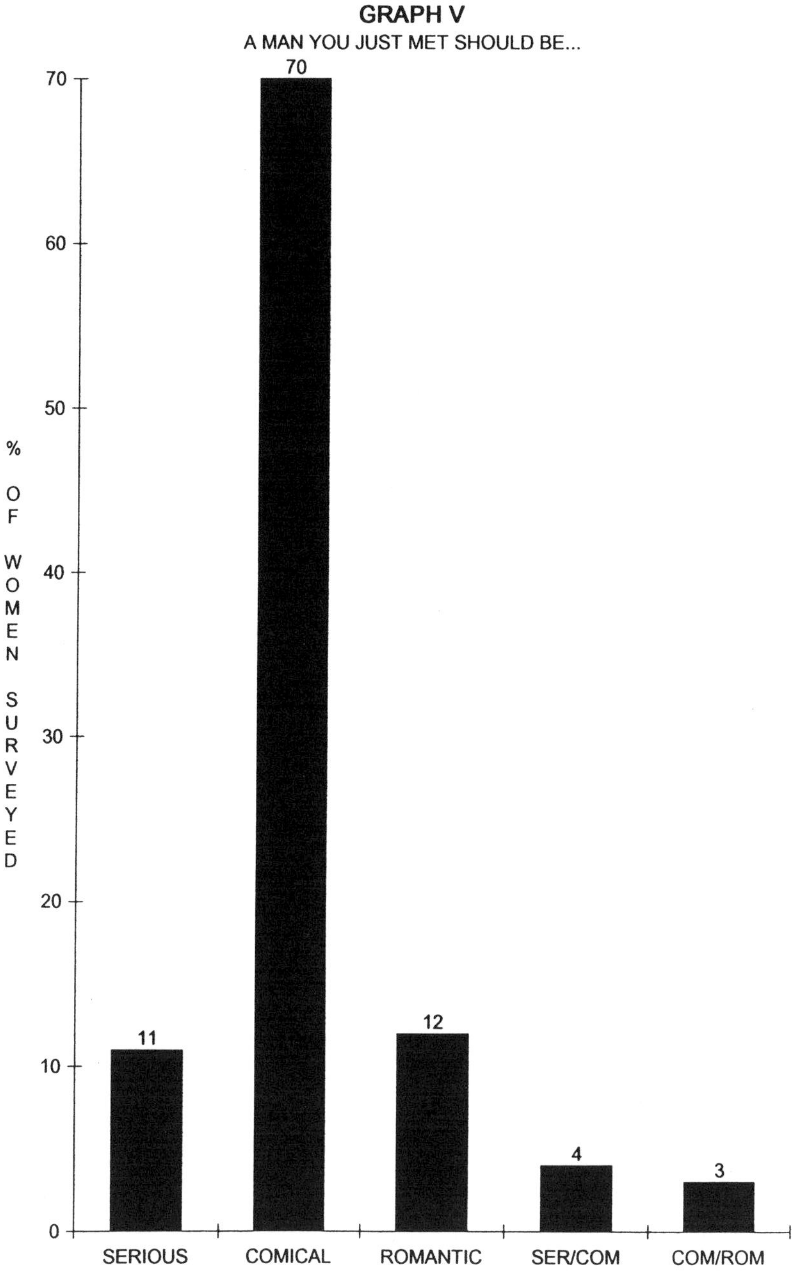

GRAPH V

A MAN YOU JUST MET SHOULD BE...

% OF WOMEN SURVEYED

	SERIOUS	COMICAL	ROMANTIC	SER/COM	COM/ROM
%	11	70	12	4	3

fashion was a pair of new construction boots." These comments don't have to be big belly laughs. They are designed to show the woman you have a sense of humor. If you are talking about alcohol and drinking, you might say, "I understand there are four levels of drinking - well five if you're a carnival worker."

A lot of times people will hit on the subject of old age. She might say, "I never want to get old and senile." You might say, "I never worry about senility - now what were we talking about?"

These are short comical phrases designed to make her laugh and add some spark to your conversation.

If you are talking about different restaurants that you like to go to, you might say, "The last time I went out to eat, I ordered the whole meal in Italian. Everyone was surprised, even the waiter. It was a JAPANESE restaurant." That one is a little longer than I would usually recommend. Try to keep your wit as short as possible and never get into actually telling a joke to the lady.

If you are talking about gambling or horse racing, you might say, "I have bad luck with horses. The ones I bet on always seem to try running on their knees." Or, "The last time I went to the casino in a $40,000 car, I came back in a $75,000 bus." Or perhaps, "I only gamble for laughs. Last time I laughed my house away."

If you are talking about people who are promiscuous, you might say, "I know people who, if they are not in bed by 10 O'Clock, they just go home."

I remember one time I was talking to two girls about drinking and driving. I said, "I don't like to drink and drive because every time I hit a bump, the drink spills all over me." They thought that was hysterical. I didn't think it was that funny, but they sure did.

If you are talking about people with money, or

people who don't have money, you could say, "Show me a guy without money, and I'll show you a bum."

If you are on the subject of old boyfriends or girlfriends you didn't like, you might want to throw in a few short jokes about the time your best friend ran away with your ex-wife (or ex-girlfriend). Then you can say, "Boy I miss him." Or you might say, "My last girlfriend is in the Congo now, teaching them how to fight dirty."

If you are talking about the band, and how bad they are, you could say, "You would not believe it, but I saw this band playing at Madison Square Garden - until the cops chased them away."

Well I hope this gives you some ideas to make the lady laugh a little and make her feel good about talking to you. I'm not a comedian, but I do have a sense of humor and it is the number one answer by a long shot. So do the best you can with your sense of humor.

"Romantic" was the second choice of beautiful women, but did not even come close to "comical." Although it was second, it only took 12% of the two thousand women interviewed. Romantic is something a woman looks forward to, usually somewhat later on in a relationship. To be romantic means to be imaginative or have some type of emotional appeal with a woman. One who is romantic is in touch with the tender feelings of a woman. For example, it's the setting where there is a fire going in the fireplace, with a bear skin rug on the floor in front of it. Just you and her in a quiet, remote log cabin; locked in a loving embrace. All your attention is focused on her alone. This is something a woman fantasizes about, somewhere down the road in a relationship, not usually when she first meets a guy.

It is a good idea to let her know that you are in favor of being romantic. That you have no problem with it.

That you like to send roses and are capable of expressing feelings, but just don't be mushy as soon as you meet her.

Third in this category was "serious." When one is serious, they are subdued. They reduce the intensity of themselves. Their appearance and manner are sedate. One gives the impression of being earnest or grave, even grim.

One is portraying that what they are doing is no laughing matter. It was very low on the scale. Most women are out to have a good time. They are not looking for someone too heavy. They want to have fun. That is why they are out in the first place.

As I stated earlier, I asked these women to add anything to the survey that they felt needed mentioning. So about four percent said they would like a guy to have a combination of "serious" and "comical," and three percent stated that they liked a man to have a combination of "comical" and "romantic" when approaching them.

QUESTION #6: WHAT IS THE FIRST THING A MAN COULD SAY TO YOU THAT WOULD MAKE YOU FEEL GOOD?

This question in the survey is so important that I devoted the next chapter to it, along with the "Top Ten Opening Approaches ." Question number 6 has a direct correlation with the "Top Ten Opening Approaches ." If you review these approximately fifty surveys, it will help give you some insight as to how these beautiful women felt about this question. We will go into it with much more depth than we have time for in this chapter. Remember, I had over two thousand surveys from which to get my information. So with all that information compiled, I decided it would take at least one whole chapter to do it justice.

QUESTION #7: WHAT WAS THE NICEST, UNUSUAL, OR FUNNIEST LINE A MAN HAS EVER TOLD YOU?

I felt this would be an interesting question for a couple of reasons. One, to see how creative and ingenious some guys can be. And, two, to get a feel for what guys think they should say when they are attracted to these women.

Here is a list of some of the best lines they have come up with. They are direct from the surveys as written.

- "Wow! Great job God!"
- "If the sky was paper and the ocean was ink, I still wouldn't be able to write down how beautiful I think you are."
- "With looks like yours, you should be in the movies."
- "Well, I'd buy you a drink, but I see you already have one. I'd ask you to dance, but I don't like to dance. So I guess I'll just strike up a conversation."
- "Your father must be a thief because he stole the twinkle from the stars and put them in your eyes."
- "What's an angel like you doing so far from heaven?"

- "Well now you've done it. I'll have to dismiss my whole harem, now that I met you."
- "Excuse me miss! Didn't we have sex once?"
- "I know you want to kiss me - what are you waiting for?"
- "My Jaguar needs an oil change - you want it?"
- "I can see right from the start - you are going to mean everything to me."
- He asked me out. I told him I had a boyfriend and he said he didn't want to take him out, just me.
- "I'd drink your bath water."
- "If I said you had a good body, would you hold it against me?!"
- "You remind me of my mother."
- "I want to fall asleep with you tonight and wake up with you in the morning."
- "Can I buy you a drink, a pack of cigarettes, a condo?"
- I was walking downstairs in a house with a huge party going on. A guy swept me off the stairs and started dancing with me, frantically spinning and turning me around. I just kind of stood there, like a blob. "Not much of a dancer, are you," he said.
- A man had his secretary ask me for a date.
- Reaction to "beautiful" perfume. I had a man follow me across a hotel to tell me how my perfume was enticing - HA - HA!
- He told me he was from a mental hospital.
- That I look like someone famous.
- "Hi - I'm drinking milk."

- "I could marry a girl like you."
- "If I wasn't with you in the end, I would want my daughter to be exactly like you."
- "You have the body of a go-go dancer."
- "I hope your friend is as good looking as you - for my friend here."
- "I may be young, but I ain't no 'Toys R Us' kid."
- "Hi - I'm related to the President."
- "I'm going to say hello even though I think you are out of my league."
- Reading a romantic passage from Oliver Twist and saying it reminded him of me.
- "You have real sexy ankles."
- "Hi, I'm alone." (aw)
- Some guy said, "Let me see your nails," grabbed my hands, and shook me to see my chest shake.
- I told a guy in a bar that I loved the song "Desperado," so he started singing it to me. (He was no Don Henley)
- When we first kissed, he said he knew it would be great when we made love. (And it was!)
- "I would take you out for dinner, but I don't have any money."
- "You know something - you're just like one of the guys."
- "I feel like we've been here before, as if I've known you all my life."
- He said, "I've been standing at attention ever since you walked into the club." I think he was referring to his private part.

- "Do you come often - I mean do you come HERE often?"
- "I wish I had a higher IQ so I could enjoy your company." (If you don't like a person, you could say, "I wish I had a lower IQ so I could enjoy your company.)
- "If I were a king, and you were my queen - we would be king and queen."
- "Do you want to change the world - how about changing mine."
- "I don't have a rare flower to give you, like they do in the movies, but could I buy you a drink anyway?"
- "It must be real sweet to be your lips."
- "I don't want to be everything to everyone, but I do want to be something to you."
- "You know, saying hello doesn't necessarily mean we'll have to say goodbye."
- "I was interested in meeting a nice girl - but I think I like you better."
- "When I saw you, I started breaking out in a cold sweat - either I love you or you're making me sick."
- "You're so pretty I could squeeze the shit out of you."
- "You know you could have something special - me!"
- "In this room full of ordinary people, I'm glad I saw you."
- "You know I used to do it three times an hour - but not since I stopped drinking beer."
- "Hi, I'm not just looking for someone, I'm looking for you."

- "In this room full of ordinary people, you are extraordinary."
- "You look like Linda Carter!"
- "You have an Italian body."
- "Are you related to Dolly Parton?"
- "Your bust is really kickin!"
- "Hi, I think we were made for each other."
- "I played this song for you."
- "I could make enough beautiful moments for you to make life seem worthwhile."
- "Hi, I wish I had a script so I would know the right thing to say to you."
- "I wish I had the requirements necessary to go out with a woman like you."
- "One of the voices in my head told me to approach you."
- "At the end of the night, we can be one step closer to knowing each other."
- "You know, on the dance floor two strangers can come together and perhaps become friends. Would you like to dance?"
- "Hi, you know when strangers' paths cross, they'll never be strangers again."
- "I've been touched by everyone in this place but you." (It was very crowded in the club.)
- "I've been touched, but I haven't been touched."
- "Your face or mine?"
- "Weren't you the nurse in that clinic I was at last week."
- "What's a horrible place like this doing around a nice girl like you."
- "4 out of 5 voices in my head recommended I come over and talk to you."

- "If I can't hold you in my arms, I can still hold you in my heart."
- "You know, even a favorable wind won't blow forever."
- "People from a planet without flowers could never send you roses."
- "You know, life is like an uncharted territory, you have to take chances."
- "It's hard to make a buck - but it would be easy to spend it on you."
- "I don't make jokes, I just watch the other guys make fools out of themselves."
- "The best relationships of all are those that haven't been made yet."
- "I think the best thing for us to do right now is talk."
- "If you had as many ideas about me as I had about you, we'd be in bed right now."
- "I could tell you a fast lie right now, or the slow truth - what do you want to hear?"
- "A life with you would be a rewarding pursuit."
- "Ya know, I came here before
and I knocked on the door
I arrived very mean
'till you came on the scene."
- "How long a minute is depends on how long it takes you to notice me."
- "I once conquered a mountain, but it wouldn't come close to conquering you."
- "I may not be right in coming over to talk to you, but you must admire my stupidity."
- "Would you mind talking to me now, because by the time I finish this drink, I'll be a slobbering idiot."

- "You know, baby, in the long run I only hit what I aim at."
- "If you let me take you to my favorite restaurant, you'd get three choices, leather, feathers, or fins."
- "You know, honey, I have a Trans Am parked outside."
- "Excuse me, did you have your U.S.D.A. recommended daily allowance of compliments today?"
- "Either I'm experiencing turbulence, or you're having a strange effect on me."
- "They say truth is stranger than fiction, that's why no one would believe you'd go out with me."
- "It's 10 O'Clock, do you know where your boyfriend is?"
- "Excuse me miss, I think your hot dog is ready."
- "I'd take my pants off over my head for you."

Those were the most unusual lines I could find in the surveys. You would be surprised how many women did not have an answer for that question. No matter how much I asked them to try to remember some nice, funny, or unusual line, they just could not come up with any. A lot of women just answered, "I have not heard it yet." Some were funny and some were unusual, but I would not advise using any of these because they are lines. They sound like lines and women don't appreciate a hard line like that. (The author of this book is not responsible for anything that happens to you as a result of using any of these lines.)

As a matter of fact, it's the last thing they want to hear now-a-days. We will go into this in more depth in the next chapter.

QUESTION #8: WHAT WAS THE NICEST COMPLIMENT A MAN HAS EVER PAID YOU?

This question coincides with question #6, "What is the first thing a man could say to you that would make you feel good?" They both lead up to what we are going to discuss in the next chapter, "Top Ten Opening Approaches Guaranteed To Work." But in the meantime, let's see what were some of the nicest compliments.

- "I'd like you to be the mother of my children."
- "Now that I have talked with you, I realize you are not only beautiful, but very intelligent."
- "You seem perfect."
- "You're great to be around - I feel good when I'm with you."
- "You are so nice to be around."
- "You are beautiful, kind, and smart."
- "Not only are you attractive, but also intelligent and sensitive."
- "You look good enough to eat."
- "You are the best looking lady I've ever seen."
- "If you had your picture taken, it would be published in a magazine."
- "You might be little, but you are perfect."
- "You have a nice shape."
- "You're a complete package."
- "You are very elegant and sophisticated."
- "You are the most intelligent woman that I have had the pleasure to go out with."

- "I wish you were flat chested and ugly so I could get a good nights sleep once in awhile, without thinking about you."
- "I wouldn't trade you for anything in the world."
- "You are a beautiful woman - your eyes can seduce me."
- "You look wonderful tonight."
- "Your boyfriend must be proud of you."
- "I would not want to be with anyone else but you."
- "You are a real lady."
- "You have a great accent."
- "If you weren't attached, I would love to go out with you."
- "You're beautiful inside and out."
- "The man you marry will be the luckiest guy in the world!"

The compliments that guys think up are usually mundane. There were countless compliments about women's eyes throughout. That was the biggest number of compliments given.

A great number of these beautiful women had to leave this question blank. I thought it was a shame that of all the guys who came into contact with these beautiful women, no one had given them a compliment that was worth remembering. I said to these women, "Come on, no one has given you a compliment on how beautiful you are?" They said if they had, they would have remembered it. The second most popular compliment was something about the nice smile they had. But most guys simply stated, "I like the way you look," and left it at that. The next biggest number of compliments mentioned something about the woman's body. After that was a compliment about how they should be a model. A lot of guys complimented women on their legs, hair, and personality.

Some mentioned how pretty or cute they thought the women were. Others told them how smart, nice, or funny they were. A few guys mentioned how they would like to spend their life with them. The biggest concern of this question was that out of the two thousand women interviewed, a lot weren't even complimented at all. So many beautiful women are going through life not even getting recognition. This is an important point to remember when we come to the "Top Ten Opening Pickup lines Guaranteed To Work" in the next chapter.

QUESTION #9: WHAT IS THE BIGGEST TURNOFF ABOUT A MAN IN YOUR OPINION?

I decided to make a graph for this question. I made a list of their comments to try and find out what the biggest turnoff about a man was to these beautiful women.

I figured if we know what really turns them off, we should simply not do it. That would solve the problem. Then when we approach a beautiful woman, we will not possess these qualities that turn them off. The number one answer that turned off these women the most was what they refer to as a guy being "full of himself." The following is how they describe a guy who is "full of himself." If any of the following statements sound like you, then stop this type of behavior immediately. Especially if you are interested in having beautiful women.

- "Being absorbed in only himself, his job, his car, and how much better 'his' is."
- "He thinks he is it."
- "Obnoxious attitude."
- "Bad attitude - I'm a stud."
- "I can use women - sleek - opinionated."
- "Conceited, absorbed in himself."
- "Thinks he's God."
- "Telling me what he has or can do - he's stuck on himself."
- "Talks about himself too much."
- "When they all think they are 'Rocky' but they are really 'Pee Wee Herman.'"
- "They think I'm interested in them for no apparent reason."
- "Big talk - never realize their shortcomings."
- "When they have that 'nobody can stop me' attitude."
- "Someone who compliments himself over and over again."
- "Bragging and being absorbed in only himself during the conversation."
- "Arrogance - one who knows it all."
- "Conceitedness, he thinks he is superior."
- "Self centered and egotistical."
- "Boasting about himself the whole time."

I'm not going to continue. There must be a million more comments just like these in the surveys, but I think you get the point with what I have given you. So, remember what the biggest turnoffs with women are, and be sure not to display any of those characteristics.

The second biggest turnoff about a man was what they called "sloppy looks." Under this category I included comments about things that they particularly didn't like. For instance, dirty fingernails was a big turnoff. So was bad odor. Other turnoffs were bad teeth and bad breath. This is how most of the comments went under the category of "sloppy looks" in their own words.

- "Any guy who has dirty fingers."
- "When he is talking to you and his breath smells."
- "I hate when a guy comes up to talk to you and he has bad body odor."
- "If he doesn't brush his teeth."
- "When he has food stuck in his teeth."
- "When he smiles and has teeth missing."
- "If he has a general messy appearance."
- "When his clothes are dirty."
- "If his hair is greasy."
- "I hate a sloppy man."
- "If he doesn't shave."
- "When it looks like he slept in his clothes."

I could go on and on with their comments, but I think you get the point. If you don't want to turn off beautiful women, try to look and be neat and clean. If you look back to question number two on the survey, you will see that women are not that picky about what you should wear. So that takes a lot of pressure off, especially if you thought you had to have all the right styles of clothes. All they are really interested in is whether the clothes you are wearing are clean and neat.

The next biggest turnoff about men was if they were "loud, aggressive, pushy, and a big show off." The word "obnoxious" had to be mentioned at least a thousand times under this category. We had better have a closer look at this word and what exactly it means, because women hate it in the men they meet. One who is "Obnoxious" causes people to have a strong dislike for them. He is contradictory to everyone and everything that is going on around him. He causes a great distaste for himself and he is antagonistic. He is inconsistent with the flow of things. He is offensive to the people around him and to the ones he meets. He is revolting to the people he comes in contact with. Let's see how that explanation coincides with some of the comments these beautiful women made about this type of guy.

- "He acts real cocky."
- "He says things to try and impress me."
- "He has a real nasty attitude."
- "When a guy is aggressively overwhelming."
- "If he has a bad temper."
- "When he talks about how much money he has."
- "When he talks so loud that everybody can hear him."
- "If he acts like a 'big man.'"
- "If he is violent."
- "When he tries to dominate the whole conversation."
- "Loud mouth."
- "Mean."
- "Puts down other people or groups of people."
- "When hc is too brazen for his own good."
- "When he is trying to be real bold."
- "When he is trying to possess you."

I hope this gives you some ideas on how NOT to act

toward the women you approach.

Number four in the category of "biggest turnoffs" was the fact that men "expected sex" from the women they just met. Here are a few comments from the women, just to give you some idea of what they meant.

- "Expecting sex or sexual responsiveness out of the first or second meeting."
- "Talks about sex too much."
- "When a man acts like an octopus."
- "When he is all over you after you just met him."
- "Asks you to have sex on the first date."
- "Tries to touch you all over, and you just met him.
- "You don't really even know him, and he wants sex."

I think it's self explanatory. I shouldn't have to go into it any further.

Fifth in this category was when a guy "swears" while he is talking to a woman. Here are a few comments about that from the women, in their own words.

- "Every other word out of his mouth is a curse."
- "Crude talk."
- "When he uses obscene language around me."
- "If he uses profanity when he is talking to me."
- "When his language is raw."
- "When he uses strong words in my presence."

I think this is pretty simple to understand. Just eliminate all harsh, crude, or obscene language from your vocabulary when speaking with these women.

Let us look at the sixth most popular turnoff, "insensitivity." I must have seen the word "rudeness" more times than I wanted to count. Let's look at some of their comments. I put the best one I could find first, it's kind of funny too.

- "Being an inconsiderate, miserable, selfish, cheapskate bastard. All of my previous mates nicely fit this description."
- "Having no respect for themselves or others."
- "Bad things to say about women."
- "When he always looks at or talks about other women in front of me."
- "He just wanted to take everything and not give anything."
- "When he does not care about my feelings."
- "If he is totally indifferent to the way I feel about things."
- "When he acts like he is 'bloodless.'"
- "If he is insusceptible to emotions about things."
- "Cold hearted."

You get the picture. Be more respectful and sensitive towards the women you approach.

Seventh in this category was "bad manners." I'm not going to go into that too deeply here. We already covered what good manners were in the survey. It was one of the top qualities women admired in a man. You might want to go over it again if you want to refresh your memory. It was the second top quality picked by these women in the first question of the interview.

Generally speaking, someone with "bad manners" is one who does not conduct himself within the social standard of politeness or in a gracious way.

Eighth in the question of "biggest turnoffs" was men who projected that "macho" image. This turned off these women and here are just a few of the statements.

- "When a guy acts like he has that macho image."
- "A real jock."
- "If a guy has an exaggerated pride in his manliness."

So, basically, if you have a strong pride in your masculinity, it is a turnoff to these women.

Ninth in this category was "being drunk." I'm not going to go into it at this point. I feel it is self explanatory.

Tenth was "lying." That is also self explanatory.

Eleventh was "smoking." I guess some girls don't like guys to smoke in their presence.

Finally, "chauvinism" was twelfth in the survey under turnoffs. These women didn't like guys who had an attitude of superiority toward them.

So, there you have it. The biggest turnoffs about men that beautiful women have revealed during the interviews. GRAPH VI will give you a look at this problem from a percentage viewpoint. There is a slight margin of error in this chart because some other turnoffs that weren't mentioned enough did not make the chart. For instance, some women mentioned materialism, weakness, and immaturity. These qualities were not mentioned enough to even make a mark on the chart. I basically stuck

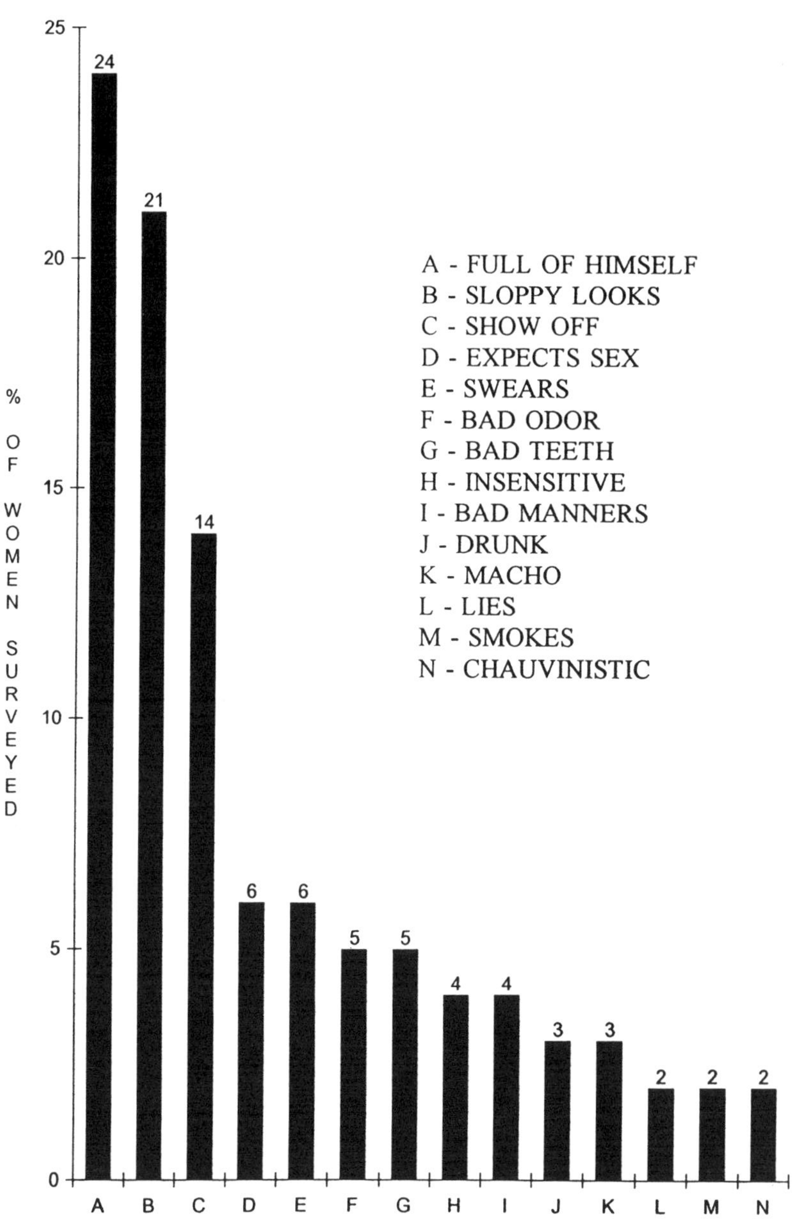
GRAPH VI
BIGGEST TURNOFF
% OF WOMEN SURVEYED
25
20
15
10
5
0
24
21
14
6
6
5
5
4
4
3
3
2
2
2
A - FULL OF HIMSELF
B - SLOPPY LOOKS
C - SHOW OFF
D - EXPECTS SEX
E - SWEARS
F - BAD ODOR
G - BAD TEETH
H - INSENSITIVE
I - BAD MANNERS
J - DRUNK
K - MACHO
L - LIES
M - SMOKES
N - CHAUVINISTIC
A B C D E F G H I J K L M N

with the biggest turnoffs that offended these women the most. If one or two women out of two thousand didn't like a particular characteristic, I figured you would be pretty busy with the other one thousand nine hundred and ninety-eight beautiful women to really worry about it.

QUESTION #10: WHAT WOULD BE THE WORST THING A MAN COULD SAY, WHEN HE FIRST APPROACHES YOU?

Now this was an interesting question. This rates as probably one of the most important points of this book. It is a direct lead in to the next chapter on "Top Ten Opening Approaches Guaranteed To Work." Not many women left this question blank. They knew what the worst thing was for a guy to say, and that is a hard "line." The biggest surprise about this question was that what these beautiful women felt was the worst thing, most guys thought was the best thing they could say when they first approached them.

Take a look at GRAPH VII so that you can get the picture on a percentage basis. These women were very precise on this point. It was almost unanimous with every woman I interviewed. These are the lines they hated the most.

- "Haven't I met you someplace before?"
- "Where have you been all my life?"
- "Don't I know you from someplace?"
- "Can I buy you a drink?"
- "Do you come here often?"
- "What's a nice girl like you doing in a place like this?"

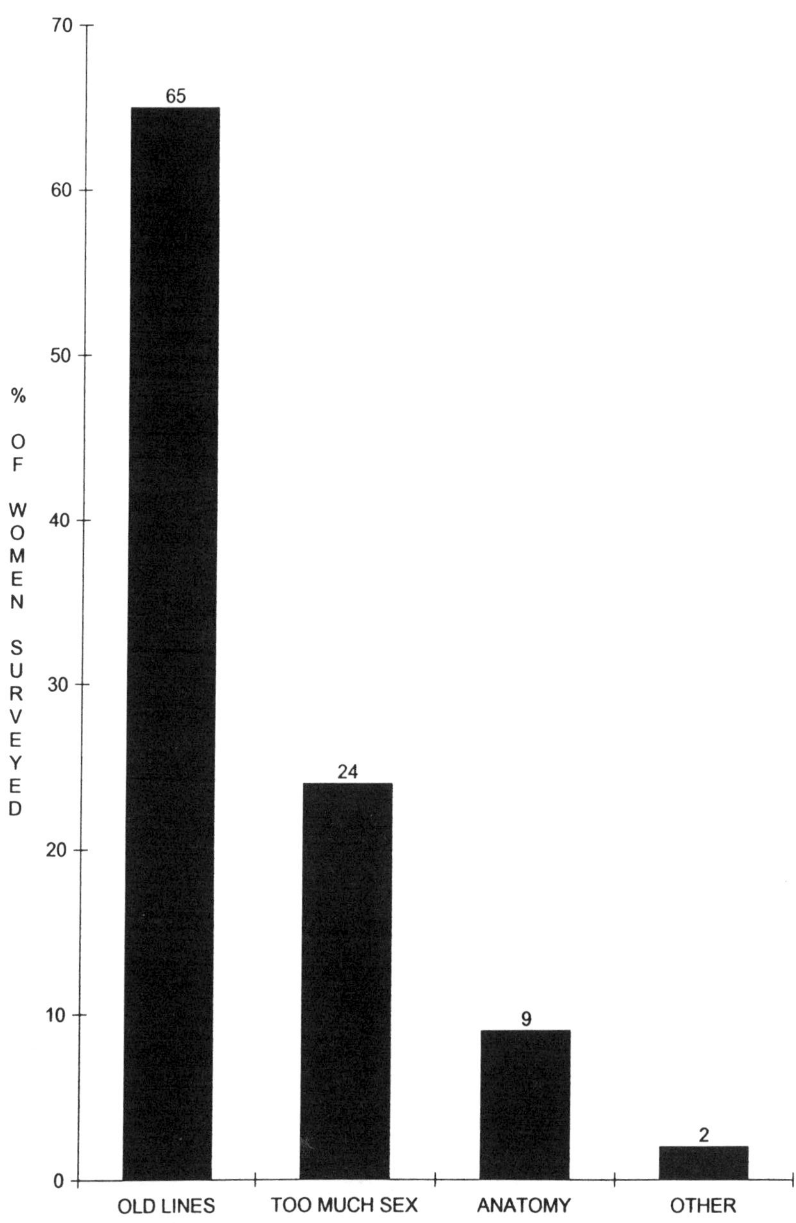
GRAPH VII
WORST THING A MAN COULD SAY
% OF WOMEN SURVEYED
70
60
50
40
30
20
10
0
65
24
9
2
OLD LINES
TOO MUCH SEX
ANATOMY
OTHER

- "Do you live around here?"
- "Hey baby, what's happening?"
- "Hey baby, what's your name?"
- "You remind me of a girl I used to know."
- "What is your sign?"
- "Do you wanna dance?"
- "Let's have a one nighter."
- "Your place or mine?"
- "Can I take you home?"
- "I would like to go to bed with you."
- "You turn me on."
- "Hey baby, what are you doing later?"
- "I like a woman with big boobs."
- "Hey, nice tits."
- "What big hooters you have."

Here are a few general comments from the women.

- "Anything that is sexual."
- "If he makes sexist comments."
- "Any mention of the anatomy."
- "Anything he says that begins with hey baby, hey babe, chick, or sweetheart."

So basically you have three categories. The first category is old lines guys have been using for too long. The second category is saying anything about having sex with these women. The third category is mentioning anything about their body parts. GRAPH VII shows you how they felt on a percentage basis.

QUESTION #11: WHAT IS THE FIRST THING YOU LOOK AT ON A MAN?

I added in this question out of curiosity. Although there is a limited amount of control over this, there still is some control in our hands.

This question is unlike the rest of the book in which we have control over what can be done to correct the situation at hand. This question affords the reader a certain amount of control, even though at first glance, it seems that there really isn't much one can do about what a woman first looks at on us.

Let me give you the first example of what I mean. The number one answer for this question was "eyes." Now you probably think there is not much you can do to change the way your eyes look. But in actuality, there is a lot you can do with your eyes. Especially that now you know this is the first thing these women look at when you approach them. First off, don't try changing the color of your eyes with contact lenses. What you can do is show your sincerity with your eyes. This is of number one importance. It is something we will discuss in depth later in the next chapter. By looking her straight in the eyes, you will be projecting honesty, another important quality these women admire. You may also show how attentive you are with your eyes. Through your eyes you can show that you are applying your mind to her and what she is talking about. They say "the eyes are the windows of the soul," so keep them clear and open.

The second choice in this category was the box labeled "other." Most women wrote in what they meant by "other." Here are a few examples.

- "I always look at his hands."
- "If he's a fun person or not."
- "I check out his smile."

- "Whether he has nice teeth or not."
- "I look at his overall appearance."
- "Hands and arms."
- "Dress and manner."
- "Shoulders."
- "What kind of face he has."

"Face" was mentioned many times, so keep it clean shaven and your hair neat.

"Hands and arms" were mentioned a lot. Try to keep your hands and fingernails clean.

Another big mention was the guy's "smile." We covered this earlier in question number three. So if you like, go over it again.

"Teeth" was another big mention. So try and keep them brushed and clean. Those were the most mentioned features under the category of "other" that these women felt were important.

"Height" was number three. If you feel you need a few extra inches, buy those boots that have big heels on them. They look nice and they add a few inches to your overall appearance. I'm five foot eight inches tall, not really what you would consider a big guy. I wear those boots with suits or jeans. They are comfortable, stylish, and add at least two inches to my overall appearance.

Very close to the number three answer, but was fourth, is "hair." We covered hair in the survey earlier. Go over it again if you would like to refresh yourself on what these women prefer. My best advice is keep it short, clean, and neat. You won't go wrong with that advice.

Number five was your "weight." Here's something most people have total control over. Remember I said most. I know some guys are very overweight and it is almost impossible to keep it under control. For those guys, don't despair. This book is designed to make the perfect guy out of you. But some guys have problems that are really out of their control. Especially if you are exceptionally overweight. But if you follow all the rest of my techniques, like other overweight guys have done, you will have no trouble getting the women you want.

I've seen it happen many times. There is definitely a barrier there when you are overweight. They are looking at that. But with the charm and charisma you'll have after mastering the techniques in this book, you will get what you want.

Basically, for the rest of you guys, try and keep any extra weight off.

The next and fifth most popular answer was "all." If a woman checked off all the answers, I just listed it under an "all" category. This basically means that this particular group of women went with an overall, general appearance of a guy. They didn't look at any particular part of a guy when he approached her. They simply had no preference for one particular thing.

"Muscles" was sixth on the scale of importance. It doesn't look like it is that important to these women. That is good, it takes a lot of pressure off of guys. Now you don't have to join a gym and sweat your balls off trying to look like Arnold Schwarzenegger.

Last was "buns." It doesn't look like it's that important either. As long as you have them, you're in.

GRAPH VIII will give you a better idea, on a percentage basis, how these women felt.

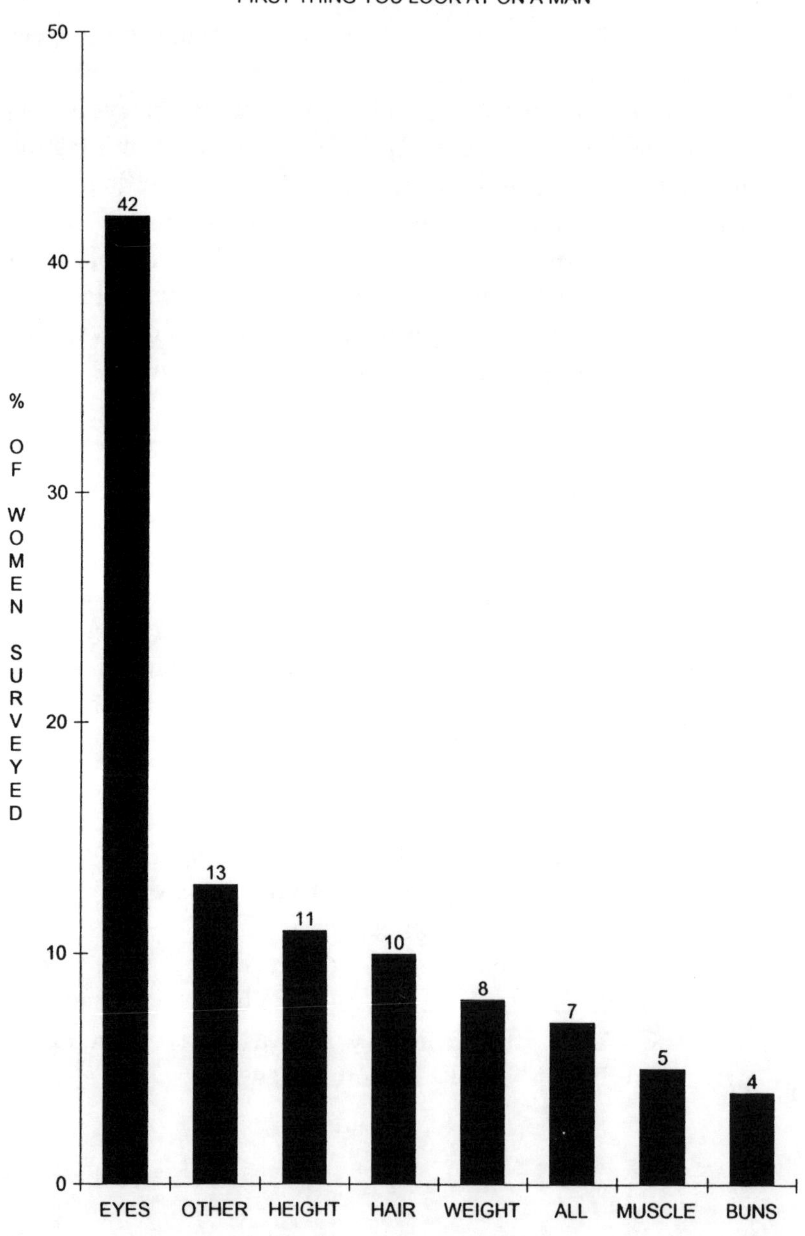
GRAPH VIII
FIRST THING YOU LOOK AT ON A MAN
% OF WOMEN SURVEYED
50
40
30
20
10
0
42
13
11
10
8
7
5
4
EYES
OTHER
HEIGHT
HAIR
WEIGHT
ALL
MUSCLE
BUNS

STUDIES

J Pers 1997 Mar;65(1):107-36

Personality and mate preferences: five factors in mate selection and marital satisfaction.

Botwin MD, Muss DM, Shackelford TK

California State University, Fresno, USA

Although personality characteristics figure prominently in what people want in a mate, little is known about precisely which personality characteristics are most important, whether men and women differ in their personality preferences, whether individual women or men differ in what they want, and whether individuals actually get what they want. To explore these issues, two parallel studies were conducted, one using a sample of dating couples (N=118) and one using a sample of married couples (N=216). The five-factor model, operationalized in adjectival form, was used to assess personality characteristics via three data sources-self--report, partner report, and independent interviewer reports. Participants evaluated on a parallel 40-item instrument their preferences for the ideal personality characteristics of their mates. Results were consistent across both studies. Women expressed a greater preference than men for a wide array of socially desirable personality traits. Individuals differed in which characteristics they desired, preferring mates who were similar to themselves and actually obtaining mates who embodied what they desired. Finally, the personality characteristics of one's partner significantly predicted marital and sexual dissatisfaction, most notably when the partner was lower on Agreeableness, Emotional Stability, and Intellect-Openness than desired.

In other words, you must have an array of socially desirable personality traits in order for a woman to find you attractive and a potential mate in life.

****

Psychol Bull 1992 Jul;112(1):125-39

Gender differences in mate selection preferences: a test of the parental investment model.

Feingold A
Department of Psychology, Yale University, New Haven, Connecticut 06520

Evolutionary-related hypotheses about gender differences in mate selection preferences were derived from Triver's parental investment model, which contends that women are more likely than men to seek a mate who possesses nonphysical characteristics that maximize the survival or reproductive prospects of their offspring, and were examined in a meta-analysis of mate selection research (questionnaire studies, analyses of personal advertisements). As predicted, women accorded more weight than men to socioeconomic status, ambitiousness, character, and intelligence, and the largest gender differences were observed for cues to resource acquisition (status, ambitiousness). Also as predicted, gender differences were not found in preferences for characteristics unrelated to progeny survival (sense of humor, "personality"). Where valid comparisons could be made, the findings were generally invariant across generations, cultures, and research paradigms.

According to this study, both men and women liked individuals who had a sense of humor and a good personality whereas women were drawn to men who have a high socioeconomic status. The higher your status, the more prestige you will have with women. I will elaborate further on this idea in the Summary.

****

J Pers Soc Psychol 1998 Oct;75(4):953-66

Sex differences in perceived controllability of mate value: an evolutionary perspective.

Ben Hamida S, Mineka S, Bailey JM

Department of Psychology, Northwestern University, Evanston, Illinois 60208, USA.

Men and women value different characteristics in potential partners. It was hypothesized that women feel they have less control over traits relevant to their desirability than men feel they have over traits related to male desirability. In Study 1, undergraduates (N=150) completed questionnaires measuring (a) the importance they attributed to 64 characteristics when choosing a mate and

(b) their perceived control over these traits. Men selected partners on the basis of traits that are relatively uncontrollable (e.g., youth, attractiveness), whereas women selected partners on the basis of traits that are more controllable (e.g., status, industriousness; d=1.75). In Study 2, these findings were replicated in an older, representative community sample (N=301; d=1.03). Greater uncontrollability of traits relevant to female mate value may place women at elevated risk for negative affect, depression, low self-esteem, and body dissatisfaction.

This study supports the basic premise of this book, that everything a woman wants, needs and desires is totally within your control, as opposed to men's selection of female traits that are uncontrollable, such as youth and attractiveness. Although women cannot control how young or attractive they are, men can control their social skill, social status, and how industrious they are in general.

6

TOP TEN APPROACHES GUARANTEED TO WORK

In this chapter you are going to learn what the basic human needs of these beautiful women are and how to fulfill them. Great psychiatrists like Sigmund Freud and philosophers like John Dewey discovered that we as human beings have, as one of our basic needs, the desire to be and feel important, special, and great. That everything we do in life is motivated from these desires. Think about your own life as an example. How many times have you ever fantasized about being special, important or great at something. These beautiful women are having the same feelings as the rest of the human race. Just think for a minute. Let's take your job for instance. Let's say your boss walked up to you and said, "I just realized, you're the greatest engineer (salesman or mechanic) in this building." You would be floored by that. Let's face it, deep down inside you've always wanted to be the greatest at what you do. Now your boss has told you so. Too bad your boss doesn't have the balls to say something like that. He never will, believe me. Even if you were the greatest at what you do. Just think how that would make you feel if you were acknowledged for that.

These TOP TEN OPENING LINES will have the same effect on the beautiful women you approach. You are going to learn how, why, and when to say these opening lines. That same basic need that great psychiatrists and philosophers have discovered in human beings, will be satisfied by you and you alone. The chemicals in that part of the brain of these women will ignite like a bolt of lightning. You will be striking and fulfilling her need to feel important, special, or great.

After using one of these opening lines, you will have instantaneously transposed this beautiful woman into a receptive individual toward you. Although this woman knew nothing about you a minute ago, she'll feel instantly good about you and what you have just said. There is nothing else you could have possibly said to her to capture her undivided attention, and put yourself in the controlling seat.

Of the two thousand women I have interviewed, every one of them said, in so many words, that they wanted to feel special by some sort of compliment. (Look at the interviews I have put into this book under question number six.)

You can start to get a feeling just from the small amount of surveys I put into this book, as to what they want. Remember, these beautiful women have spent hours getting themselves ready to go out for the evening. I mean actual hours working on themselves to look as beautiful as they do. When they finally arrive at the club, they spend more time in the ladies room touching up the last fine details of their make-up that may have smudged or worn off from the ride in the car. They re-fix their hair again. They're doing all this so someone will appreciate how special they have made themselves. Remember, you are not meeting these women, at this time, on an intellectual level. You are meeting these women on an emotional and "feelings" level.

I will let you in on a few more secrets. The only way that any of these opening lines will work is if they are said sincerely. These lines have to come from the heart, not through the teeth. They have to be said with feeling.

If I could tell you what the lottery numbers were going to be next week, you'd play them, wouldn't you? If I could tell you what horse was going to come in first tomorrow, you'd bet on it, wouldn't you? You bet you would. Well, I don't know what lottery numbers will be picked or which horse will come in first, but I do know how to open the hearts of beautiful women, no matter what color or nationality they may be.

By the way, these surveys were taken by the same percent of white and non-white women that is equal to the population of the country.

Of the two thousand surveys, and all the beautiful women I have met over the last twenty-three years, it is unanimous. These top ten opening lines will open their hearts to you, if said sincerely.

When you see a beautiful woman, you should wholeheartedly feel it. Let's face it, she is beautiful, so you should sincerely feel that she is. You should really "feel it" when you say one of the opening lines.

A big percent of these stunningly beautiful women, who had sex practically dripping off of them, had no answer for question number eight in the last chapter (What is the nicest compliment a man has ever paid you?). It seems hard to imagine that no one has ever told them how beautiful they were, or even complimented them. Imagine what awaits the man who knows what to say to these women.

If, for some reason, you can't say these opening lines sincerely, I will let you in on another secret. When a great actor has to do a romantic scene in a movie, his greatness is based on how believable and sincere he appears to be when he says his lines. For that moment when he says his lines to the female actress, he is, for all intent and purposes, feeling what he is saying. If he is telling her how much he loves her, for that moment, he is actually feeling genuine love for that actress. This is what separates a great actor, sought after with millions of dollars by Hollywood, from a low paid actor, doing "B" movies. Those actors are making millions getting you to believe what they are saying. What you'll get will be worth more than millions, if you say these opening lines sincerely.

It may be something you have to practice, almost like great actors practice and rehearse their lines at home the night before the scene.

You have to actually feel the emotions you are expressing at the moment you are expressing them. Above all, do not be mushy when you are saying one of the opening lines. Sincerity is in, mushy is out.

When Clint Eastwood told that guy, who was about to shoot that defenseless woman, "Go ahead, make my day," (remember that line, who could forget it) Clint was actually capable of killing that person at that moment. His feelings were no different than had he actually been in that same situation in real life. That is what separates him, and other great actors, from the mediocre actors. That is why he has been one of the top actors, sought after by Hollywood for most of his career.

This is the same thing you'll have to learn to enhance your expression of sincerity. Especially if you have trouble saying these opening lines sincerely.

Never use any old pickup lines. Use question Number 10 in the previous chapter as a reference as to what *not* to say. These beautiful women are fed up with hearing those worn out lines. You'll have to dig yourself out of a hole for the next ten minutes if you use one of those lines. It is the fastest way to turn off these women. It makes them feel like you are taking them for idiots when you try to use an old line on them. They know all those old lines, they have heard them a thousand times before, and they don't want to hear them again.

The first thing that comes out of your mouth has to make her feel good. It is like unlocking an emotional door in her mind, which gives you the privilege of passing through.

Let me give you an example of how this technique works.

An extremely beautiful woman, with sandy blond hair, perfect features, beautiful blue eyes, tall, with measurements of about 36" - 24" - 36", had been coming into a club I worked in. She usually stayed within a group of about twenty people that knew each other. I was going to approach her, but they always came in when it started to get busy and they sat at the tables. I was thinking about taking a break to go and meet her, when she happened to approach the bar seeking a match. Now was my chance. She simply said to me, "Do you have matches behind the bar?" I said, "Of course we do." As I struck the match and started to light her cigarette, I looked her straight in the eyes and said, "I've been watching you for weeks, and I just want you to know, you are the most beautiful woman who has ever come into this room."

I said it as sincerely as I possibly could. Whenever I said this to a woman, I really felt that way about her. So I really wasn't faking it. There was no way she could sense anything wasn't genuine in what I was saying because, for all intent and purposes, I actually felt that way.

She was stunned and said slowly, "Well - thank you very much." As I was handing her the matches, I held the back of her hand with my left hand and I placed the matches in her palm with my right hand, saying, "My name is John. It's a great pleasure to finally get to meet you. Will you come back over the next time you need a drink? I'd like to make it for you and talk to you a little." She agreed. I knew from that moment on, she couldn't think of anything else but what I had just said to her. I spotted her looking at me periodically while I was working. It wasn't because she thought I was irresistibly handsome, believe me. So I just bided my time until she came back and asked me to make her a drink. After we went out a few times, she admitted that no one had ever complimented her like that before in her life. She didn't have to tell me that. I already knew. That was years ago, and I can guarantee that no one has ever complimented her like that since. The way I approached her is something she will never forget for the rest of her life. She'll remember every detail about that night because it made her feel so good and so important. The whole world stopped for her while I looked into her eyes and said those elusive words as sincerely as I could.

I knew that the guy she was seeing at the time never said anything like that to her. I've always felt, "If you didn't have the brains or the balls to say things like I did to women, then you don't have the brains or the balls to keep them either."

A woman will never forget the first thing you say to her. No matter what you say from that time on, the first thing you said will go around and around in her mind. Just look at question number ten in the last chapter.

None of these women forgot what the worst thing was that a man said when he first approached her. So it is the most important thing you can do.

Here is a list of the TOP TEN OPENING LINES GUARANTEED TO WORK, (not only by me, but by thousands of women interviewed) when said ***sincerely.***

1 It's never easy meeting a complete stranger, especially one as beautiful as you, without being properly introduced, but shall we try anyway?

2 Hi, a beautiful woman like you should have a great evening, give me a chance to let that happen. May I join you in a drink?

3 Hi, I just wanted to tell you that what you are wearing looks stunning on you. May I join you?

4 I'm not trying to be rude or impolite, or invade your space in any way, I just wanted to know if a lovely girl like you can use some pleasant company?

5 Hi, I was hoping a beautiful woman like you wouldn't mind if I came over to talk to her. May I join you?

6 I've never really said this to anyone before, but I just felt I had to tell you - you're the most beautiful woman I've ever seen.

7 I was intrigued by your beauty and grace, and I just couldn't keep myself from coming over. May I join you in a drink?

8 Hi, I just couldn't wait a minute longer to tell you how lovely I think you are. May I join you in a drink?

9 Hi, I've seen that king of dress on other women, but none of them looked as great as you do in it. Do you mind if I join you?

10 As I was standing there, I noticed how beautiful you were. I thought perhaps we could spend our time more agreeable together. May I join you?

Once you have approach a woman and complimented her with one of these top ten opening lines, ask her, "May I join you?" and don't wait for her to answer the question. That would give her too much time to think about it. Don't give her mind a chance to start an intellectual process. As you say, "May I join you?," imply that you are going to join her. After a compliment like the one you just paid her, she is feeling quite good about you already. Try not to make it sound contrived. You may replace the word "beautiful" with any complimentary adjective you feel comfortable with. Remember how important it is for her to get the "vibe" that what you just said came from your heart. She wants to hear more of what you've got to say that will make her feel good and important.

It must be spontaneous. Her mind is now in the "yes" mode from your compliment. If you actually give her time to think about it, you will lose the edge. It must be a smooth process. After you say, "May I join you?," extend out your hand without a pause and say, "My name is *so-and-so,* and your name is?" Then you say, without hesitation, "You know, I really meant what I said. There was just no other way of telling you other than coming right out with it." That is enough about that - you stated that she was beautiful, but not in a mushy way. You told her how sincere you felt about it. Now let that sink in while you start your conversation. Then, without waiting, find a subject you both may know something about, such as the latest movies, recent news, or the music the band is playing. Try to keep it light. Follow that with what she does for a living or the kind of car she drives. Keep this conversation about her. Keep making her feel important and special. If you're worried that you are not good looking enough, don't. The charm and charisma you are projecting is reaching her far deeper than the trivial wants she may have for an extremely good looking guy. And above all, during the course of the conversation, project yourself as a human being that is capable of having feelings. Don't be afraid to show her that you have feelings. They are looking for that now-a-days. Once she starts talking about herself, you don't have to worry about keeping the conversation going. It may, and probably will, get a little boring to you at this point. Never let her know that.

Let her talk about herself, no matter how boring it may seem. After awhile, start using your power of persuasion, which you have developed from Chapter 2.

Remember, we communicate with each other through words. You can acquire anything you want from people if you know how to use the right words. So, you are going to have to learn to use these words to your advantage.

These techniques work extremely well with attractive women just as they do with beautiful women, if not better. There have been numerous occasions when I have been out and there weren't any beautiful women available. Attractive women have an even stronger need to feel beautiful, because they are working so hard to look that way. The man who appreciates this by using one of my opening lines, as well as the rest of the techniques, will do extremely well.

As I stated earlier, these techniques work anywhere you see a beautiful woman. It doesn't have to be in a nightclub or a restaurant. If you see a beautiful woman walk by, you simply start by saying, "Excuse me, I don't want to seem rude or impolite, but as you walked by I couldn't help noticing how beautiful you were. I understand this may be a bit awkward for you. Especially because we have not been properly introduced, but there really was no other way for me to tell you, other than walking right up to you. I hope you'll excuse my boldness, but I feel it would be a real tragedy if I let a great opportunity like this pass by." By the way, women respect a man that won't pass up a great opportunity. Especially when it is *them* that is being considered the great opportunity.

Never pausing, you continue by saying, "If you're not married or really serious about someone, I think we could spend some time more agreeably together. People have to meet each other, even if it's under circumstances like this. If you have a few minutes you can spare, would you mind spending them on me?"

"My name is *so-and-so.*" At this point, you reach out your hand just as you do if you were meeting her in a nightclub and say, "And you are?" She will tell you her name and without hesitation you will continue with the techniques outlined in this book. Never give her time to make a negative decision about you.

When you are in the mall, on the beach, or at the boardwalk, she probably will not be inclined to leave with you. Remember, I said "probably." You never know what she will do until you ask. But, don't push the issue and don't ask until you have had a nice conversation with her and she feels comfortable with you. If you used the techniques in this book and you ask for her phone number, she will give it to you. The next time you call her, she will go out with you and you can take it from there.

Remember, never lie about yourself or what you do for a living. Women of today are practical people. They can take care of themselves. They are not after your money. Their only concern is whether your job has a future or not. So look them straight in the eye and be truthful. If you follow these techniques, especially the Super Techniques in the Summary of this book, every time you see a beautiful woman, you will be amazed at the results.

There's a whole new set of rules today. Let me try to summarize some important ones for you.

☞ ***RULE I: TAKE ALL YOUR OLD LINES AND THROW THEM IN THE TRASH CAN.*** It's the worst thing you can say when you first approach these beautiful women. Use one of my opening lines outlined in this chapter. It takes a beautiful woman much work and effort to look the way she does. With one of these opening lines, you will be complimenting her in an intelligent way and appreciating the fact that she worked so hard to look so beautiful.

☞ ***RULE II: "SINCERITY" IS IN, "MUSHY" IS OUT.*** Make sure what you say to her is done in a sincere way. Be as sincere as possible throughout your encounter. Don't be soft or weakly sentimental.

☞ ***RULE III: TAKE ALL YOUR "BULLSHIT" AND THROW IT INTO THE TRASH CAN.*** Women today are sick and tired of "bullshit." Let's take your job for instance. As long as you have a job with a future, that's all she is concerned about. You don't have to act like you have a lot of money or are the president of a prestigious company.

☞ ***RULE IV: THE WOMEN OF THE MILLENNIUM ARE NOT "GOAL ORIENTED."*** Being "Goal Oriented" is a guy thing. I understand that because I'm a guy. That is why I wrote this book. If "D" is having the beautiful woman of your dreams, then I'll show you "A," "B," and "C." That is exactly how we (guys) want things laid out. That's how I would want information laid out for me, and that's exactly how I have given you the information. Women, on the other hand, are looking for a nice relationship to develop eventually. She is not concerned with the "immediate." She is thinking into the future.

☞ ***RULE V: SHOW THE WOMEN THAT YOU ARE CAPABLE OF HAVING FEELINGS.*** No woman wants to talk to a piece of granite. I know it's not easy for a guy to show feelings, however, if that's what they want, then that's what we should try to do. Your conversation with a women should have more familiarity and informal warmth. Ask open ended questions and learn to share your feelings and emotions with her during your conversation. In other words, let her know there is a real person in there.

☞ ***RULE VI: DELETE FROM YOUR PERSONALITY THE BIGGEST TURNOFFS STATED BY THESE BEAUTIFUL WOMEN.*** Take a look at question number nine in Chapter 5 to refresh your memory. There are nine really big turnoffs that you should stay as far away from as possible.

☞ ***RULE VII: INCORPORATE INTO YOUR PERSONALITY THE BIGGEST TURN ONS FROM THE INTERVIEWS.*** Look over all the turn ons throughout the questions in Chapter 5, and make sure you have these positive attributes.

☞ ***RULE VIII: YOUR APPEARANCE IS VERY IMPORTANT TO THESE BEAUTIFUL WOMEN.*** Go over the previous chapter and review the questions on what she expects you to look like when you first approach her.

☞ ***RULE IX: YOU MUST PROJECT A "SAFE" IMAGE.*** No matter what the circumstances are, always make her feel safe. Look over the chapter on persuasion for more information.

☞ ***RULE X: STOP WORRYING ABOUT REJECTION.*** The next chapter is going to alleviate all your anxieties about rejection.

This book gives you an in-depth understanding about the women of the millennium, what she's all about, and where she's coming from.

I interviewed over two thousand beautiful, available women who are out there waiting right now. Their responses are universal. They are out there waiting for the guy who knows what they want. What they want is a guy who fits the description in the interviews. Remember, it comes straight from their own beautiful mouths, so "he who fits the mold, gets the beautiful women."

STUDIES

What men and women compete for:

There was a study done at King's College Research Centre, Cambridge, UK, in which they wanted to determine what men and women compete over. The study used competition diaries to see whether "men and women differ in (a) what they compete over, (b) whom they compete with, and (c) their competitive tactics including use of aggression. In study one, university students kept diaries of their competitive interactions during the term. Sex differences were as follows: (a) men's diaries contained more same sex competition, (b) women competed more about ***looking attractive*** *whereas men competed more about sports and (c) men used physical (but not verbal) aggression more frequently than women. In Study two, strength of competition was also measured by questionnaire. Women and men felt equally competitive overall, but men felt more competitive about athletics and sexual attention whereas women felt more competitive about* ***looking attractive****. In men, but not women, competitiveness for financial success was correlated with various aspects of mating competition. Young men were more competitive than older men in a variety of domains and were also more physically and verbally aggressive, but no age difference in aggression was found for women."**

It is obvious from this study, women are predominantly competing with each other for attention concerning their looks, more than anything else. By using my top ten pick up lines, you will tap into that resource by reinforcing the fact that they do look beautiful. When you approach women in the way I have outlined in this chapter, it will make them feel that they are more attractive than anyone else, which is their ultimate goal and that you were the one who recognized it. Having this insight will give you a great advantage when trying to get a date with a beautiful woman. Approaching a woman and making her feel beautiful will set you on the right path. One can also determine from the study that no matter how old or young the women are they still compete when it comes to looking attractive.

**Br J Soc Psychol 1998 Jun;37 (pt 2):213-29*

****

J Pers Soc Psychol 1985 May;48(5):1191-203

Telling ingratiating lies: effects of target sex and target attractiveness on verbal and nonverbal deceptive success.

DePaulo BM, Stone JI, Lassiter GD

Male and female "senders" described their opinions on four controversial issues to target persons. Each sender expressed sincere agreement with the target on one of the issues and sincere disagreement on another (truthful messages), and also pretended to agree with the partner on one of the issues (an ingratiating lie) and pretended to disagree on another (a noningratiating lie). Groups of judges then rated the sincerity of each message on the basis of information available from one of four different channels: verbal (words only, in transcript form), audio (audiotape only), visual (videotape with no sound), and audiovisual (videotape with sound). Results showed that (a) lies told by women were more readily detected than lies told by men, (b) lies told to opposite-sex targets were more easily detected than lies to same-sex targets, and (c) ingratiating lies were more successfully detected than were noningratiating lies, particularly when told to attractive targets, Furthermore, when senders talked to opposite-sex (relative to same-sex) targets, their lies were most easily detected from the three channels that included nonverbal cues. For ingratiating (relative to noningratiating) lies, detectability was greatest for the channels that included visual nonverbal cues. Senders addressing attractive targets were perceived as less sincere than senders addressing unattractive targets, both when lying and when telling the truth, and this difference in the degree of sincerity conveyed was especially pronounced in the channels that included nonverbal cues. Results are discussed in terms of the effects of motivation on verbal and nonverbal communicative success.

After contemplating this study, go back over section (c) regarding ingratiating lies (which are lies designed to bring oneself into the favor of another). These lies were more successfully detected when told to attractive women. That is why, in this chapter, I stress that you are as sincere and truthful as possible when using the Top Ten Pick Up Lines Guaranteed To Work. I hope this sheds more light on the power of sincerity.

7

REJECTION

Rejection. What is it? Why do we fear it so much? Most people would rather be marched out in front of a firing squad than face rejection by the opposite sex. Let us look at how the dictionary defines rejection. They use words like "eliminate, shut out, exclude, throw out, unsatisfactory." All cold, hard words which we don't want to deal with. We don't want anyone to feel this way about US! Especially someone who is the object of our affections. The best defense against this problem is knowledge.

This book gives you everything you could possibly need to know about approaching the opposite sex. So why have the anxiety of feeling rejected anymore. You are now armed with everything you need to avoid rejection. Just try the techniques outlined in this book, with one of the opening pickup lines, and the probability of being rejected will be next to nothing.

FORCE YOURSELF

Sometimes we have to force ourselves to approach a beautiful woman the first few times. Even if it is against our own will. That is the only way you will find out that these techniques really work. You can read this book and study the techniques. But when you see that beautiful woman sitting there, and anxiety comes over you, that is the time to get up and use these techniques. No matter what you are unsure of, this is the only way. No one can do it for you.

After you approach a few beautiful women, and you see the reaction you are getting, all that anxiety will disappear and you will be relaxed and confident.

As men we have to depend on our reason. If there is a problem, we must figure out how to solve it. We can't hope everything will work out. We must know exactly how to MAKE things work out. A lot of reason, and a little courage, is all we need to succeed.

BE CONFIDENT

All your doubts will disappear once you know that the outcome will be success. Confidence is a very respectful quality in a man. Confidence will overpower any anxiety or fear of rejection you may be having when you see a beautiful woman whom you want to approach.

There was a point in my life that I would say to myself, when I spotted a beautiful woman, she has no idea at this time that she'll be having a relationship with me. Then I would approach her, knowing that this will transpire at my will. Once you master the contents of this book, you will be saying the same thing to yourself. All your fears will dissipate and total confidence will emerge. The faith in yourself, and the mastery of these techniques, will give you that bold fearless air about yourself.

FIGHT OR FLIGHT

Anxiety and adrenaline were useful in the caveman era. They would help him survive during a time when he had to confront all sorts of beasts and other cavemen. Although modern man still has to survive, we don't have to face violent circumstances. But we do have to face other types of anxiety, unless we just stay at home and never go out and get what we want. So, we therefore must face the anxiety of being rejected. We can reduce the high level of anxiety and use the normal amount of anxiety that is left, in a positive way.

TAKE IT STEP BY STEP

Look at it as an adventure. If you never approached a beautiful woman before, go slowly. Just use one of the opening pickup lines when you approach, say a few things, and leave. This is just to see what kind of open reception you'll get. Practice that a few times until you see how receptive a beautiful woman can be when you say the right things to her.

This will increase your confidence each time. Don't just put this book down without trying the techniques. I don't care what you look like or how old (or young) you are. These techniques will definitely work. Look at me.

I'm an average looking guy with an oversized nose and scars on my face from acne I'd had when I was a teenager. Yet, I know for a fact that I can have any beautiful woman, who is single, anytime I want. It is not what you look like at all, it is what you know and how you use it.

A lot of men have turnoff mechanisms in their brains. Once an anxiety situation arises, they simply turn off to the situation and avoid it. This resolves the conflict in their mind and relieves them of all anxiety. But it doesn't get them anything.

A LITTLE ANXIETY CAN HELP

Let's become aware of what is causing this anxiety. With the anxiety of being rejected, we feel threatened that the beautiful woman will not want us. So, this is a conflict going on within us. We know what we want, but we are afraid we may be turned down. Educating ourselves on how to overcome the problem is the only realistic way to solve it. Remember, a little anxiety can help. It is not always bad. There is no such thing as a life totally without anxiety. Everyone has anxiety, but some of us know how to use it in a positive way. We have to confront what is causing the anxiety. Don't avoid the anxiety-causing situation, and don't try to go around it either. Use the determination of what you want as a motive. What you are going to achieve will be much better than how you are going to feel, if you let it pass by. Just think how satisfied you will be when you realize the new power you are developing. By not using my techniques, you are forfeiting the expansion of many relationships with beautiful women that will enrich your life. The price you pay for giving into anxiety is horrible compared to what you will achieve by boldly facing it.

TOO MUCH ANXIETY

When we let anxiety take over, there is no productivity. Everything becomes vague. We don't think right. We are not original. We are not even in touch with reality. All logic is blurred, our heart rate goes up, our pulse rate goes up, and we become irrational. We become paralyzed in our thinking capacity.

Remember, people who don't try anything in their life face little anxiety. But creative, intelligent people face anxiety because that is the only way for someone to accomplish anything. Plus, the intelligent person uses anxiety to help them perform better. That's right, anxiety can actually help you instead of hinder you, as long as it is a moderate amount.

The problem with people who have too much anxiety is that what they expect is going to happen, and what *really* is going to happen, are two completely different things. But, in your case, the anxiety should be at a normal level. A level that should help you, because what you expect to happen is actually what will happen. You will gain a new freedom in your life. Your creativity will develop in areas you never dreamed of.

HOW MEN HANDLE REJECTION

Let us look at how some men have handled.rejection in their lives. Most men are so fearful of being rejected that they won't even admit it happened to them. We have a mechanism inside us that goes off, and we won't even discuss the fact that we have been rejected. We don't even hear when someone might be rejecting us. We just continue to be persistent no matter how badly we are doing with the woman. Before this book, men really did not understand women that well, and they would be shattered when a woman turned them down. No matter how many subtle hints a woman would give a guy, he would simply not hear any of them, until he would finally get a flat "no" from the female.

Other men have different ways of dealing with rejection. They believe that when they see a beautiful woman, she is automatically seeing another man. They think the worst is going to happen. They are ready to be rejected BEFORE they even begin to get started. Some men think that women are brought up to say no, that it's some kind of instinct a woman has. This also gets them ready to be rejected before they even get started.

A lot of guys won't directly ask a woman out on a date. They will say things like, "Maybe we could get together sometime for lunch, or something," just to see whether she will reject that idea or not. If she agrees, this will tell the guy whether or not he can take the next step.

I AM BETTER THAN HE IS

I remember a time when I put myself in a situation where rejection was imminent. I was at my friend Tom's house, when his girlfriend, Alysia, and her girlfriend, Kathy, stopped over before going shopping. Kathy was so unbelievably beautiful, that I was stunned at the sight of her. When we were introduced, I could hardly contain my blood pressure. I was trying to appear calm as I told her how beautiful I thought she was. After they left, I asked Tom why he never told me about her. He told me she was engaged to be married within a year. I said, "I don't care if she is getting married, I just want to go out with her a few times." I asked his girlfriend to give me her address. She agreed, and I sent Kathy a dozen roses with a small note in it. The note said how beautiful she was, and I also wrote, "I am better than he is." I did not say at what, I just said "I was better." I left that part up to her imagination.

I didn't ask her out, because she had no choice but to say "no" at this point. I told her that the roses were simply a token of my admiration for her. Each time we met, I would reinforce the fact that I thought she was so beautiful, and sent her another dozen roses. I still did not ask her out. I knew at this time she would still have to say "no." Especially since she was going to get married eventually. But, I still left the note, "I am better than he is," in with the roses.

After several of these gestures, and an actual friendship emerged, I decided that I had broken her down enough not to reject me. Seeing as I was always around Tom and Alysia when they were with Kathy, we became a tight group.

I then decided to ask her to let me prove that "I was better than he was," still not saying at what; just leaving it up to her imagination. "Besides," I said, "this is the last time you ever get to go out with another man, now that you are going to get married. It will be like a last fling or something. You'll never get this chance again."

"Besides," I told her, "it is only going to be some dancing and a few drinks at a nice club. I promise your fiancé will never ever find out about it." She had her reservations about it, but finally agreed to go out with me. Well, we had a fun time together, if you know what I mean. She did marry that guy, and believe me, I wanted her to marry him. And everybody lived happily ever after, I think. At least I did.

The point is that anyone can turn any rejection around if he knows how to approach it. We tend to take rejection like a stake in the heart. As if it were so final, but it doesn't have to be.

IT'S LIKE A BUSINESS TRANSACTION

A lot of guys who want a date with a woman feel they are being rejected if the woman says she is busy at the time he wants to go out. They hang up the phone and never call again, thinking they have been rejected. I would say most of the time this is not a rejection. That the woman actually is busy at that time. You have to communicate more with the woman. If it were a business deal, you would not hang up without finding out what you could do to make the deal. You would communicate the best you know how to make the buck. You would make other arrangements to meet with a business partner, no matter what it took you to do it.

So, what is the difference when you want a woman. Why do we accept rejection so easily when it comes from the opposite sex. Find out why she can't make it on the day you wanted to go out. Then, make arrangements for a different time. If she is still not available, find out what the problem is and whether you two can work it out.

RELEASING THE PAIN

As men, we don't have a way of expressing our pain. We are supposed to be too macho for that. So we keep it pent up inside. Whereas women have avenues to release these feelings. She can show her feelings to other people and release the pain. For a woman, rejection is not the end of the world. But for men it is like the end of the world, because we have to live with these feelings of rejection inside of us, with no way out.

SOME POSSIBILITIES OF REJECTION

You have to remember that when someone rejects you, not to take it so personally. Most of the time, the person doing the rejecting does not know you well at all. If they just knew what kind of a person you really were, they would not be rejecting you. If you keep this in mind, it will make it easier if this happens to you.

The woman might be married and doesn't want her husband to know that she is going out. She might be so much in love with another man, that going out with you is simply out of the question at this point. Or it may be even simpler than that. I know of so many times when a guy would ask a woman to dance, and she would say no. The guy would take this as a rejection and walk away. After I questioned the woman as to why she did not dance with the guy, she would say, "I just did not feel like dancing right now. That's all." But the guy thought this meant that she did not want to have anything to do with him. Which, as you can see, was not the case.

I cannot begin to tell you how many times a guy would try to buy a lady a drink from across the bar. If she refused the drink, the guy would immediately take this as a rejection and completely turn off to her for the rest of the night. But, when I questioned the lady as to why she did not take the drink, she would reply by saying, "I did not want another drink," or simply, "I don't know." But, again, the guy thought that this was a rejection for some reason that only he knew in his mind. It had nothing to do with reality at all. She simply did not want a drink, or just did not know why she didn't want a drink, at that moment.

I have seen thousands of guys think they were getting rejected in my time. Had they known the techniques outlined in this book, they could have gotten what they wanted, instead of going home empty handed or settling for something less.

They say the worst thing to do about rejection is not to face it or deal with it. Once one confronts it, the pain will be over faster. Some guys find a new partner right away, just to keep their mind off of the last rejection.

Sometimes a rejection can be a good thing. Especially if it is an ongoing relationship that is just not working out. It gives the two people a chance to start anew with someone else. Someone they get along with better.

YOU DO IT - I DO IT

Everyone gets rejected at some time or another. Even you have rejected people for some reason in life. It didn't mean that the person you rejected was no good. It just meant that you did not want what they were offering at that point in your life. You may want it at some other point, but just not right now. The same thing has happened to all of us. Unless you are not from this planet Earth, you probably will have to face some form of rejection. I am not saying that being rejected by someone else is not going to make you feel sad and down in the dumps a little. But don't let it go any further than that. Deal positively with your feelings. Pull up that self-esteem a little and try again.

It is probably their problem anyway, not yours. Don't take rejection as gospel, it's just a problem that *they* are having. Even children in a playschool situation learn that rejection doesn't mean the end of the world. If they keep trying to play with a group of kids, eventually they will be accepted into the group. A little assertiveness can go a long way.

TURNING AROUND REJECTION

I remember a time when my buddy was in a situation of being rejected but turned it around to his advantage. There was this pretty blond named Betty that apparently liked a bartender named Dan. Dan had some plastic surgery on his nose, lips, and chin and was a good looking guy. Bob, another bartender, wanted Betty, but she rejected him for Dan. Dan, on the other hand, did not want Betty.

I asked Dan why he did not want Betty, and he just did not know. So Bob bided his time. He did not take the rejection as gospel. He just thought he wasn't what she wanted at that time, and he was right. Although Betty tried to pursue Dan, he still didn't want her. When Betty finally got the idea that Dan was not going to budge, she gave up. Now Bob tried his hand again. He wasn't quite as good looking as Dan but still had the perseverance. His perseverance paid off because he eventually got Betty and what he wanted.

You see, it wasn't that Betty really didn't want Bob. She just didn't want him at that point in her life. But at another point, he was just perfect for her. It is a classic case of someone taking a situation that looks like a total rejection and turning it around.

YOU HAVE THE POWER OF CONTROL

Remember, you have the power to control your rejections and how you feel about them. Other people might be responsible for causing the rejection, but only you control how you feel afterwards. Don't think that because one person does not want what you have, that no one will. It may be that they don't want it now. They might want it at some future time. Do not think that if there is something someone does not like about you, that you are totally no good. Never blame yourself totally for the rejection either. It takes two people to cause a rejection.

BACK TO YOUR CHILDHOOD

They say some people are more susceptible to the pain of rejection than others. A lot has to do with the way we were brought up. Whether our parents told us we were never going to get anyplace in life or not during our childhood. This susceptibility lowers our self-esteem. When we get rejected, we think we are "no good" anyway and the pain runs deeper.

Think about the last time you were rejected. What were your thoughts? A lot were irrational. Irrational thoughts about yourself that had no basis of who you really are. If you think about it now, in a rational way, you will find that most of those thoughts had nothing to do with reality. You should now replace those irrational thoughts with real, positive thoughts about yourself to see where your thinking goes wrong immediately after a rejection.

NEVER THINK THE WORST

Don't be so hard on yourself. Nobody but God has the right to judge you as a human being. Don't ever expect to be rejected by someone. This can only make it worse for you, especially if the rejection really comes. Try to build up confidence little by little. Some people have to go a little slower than others when building up confidence. But going in with the idea that you are going to be rejected will most likely be detected by the person you are approaching. You must have the air of confidence in order to win over the person you approach. There is nothing worse than approaching someone with a timid, shy, self defeating sort of attitude.

We have all been rejected at one time or another in our life, but we all survived it. We are still here. It is not all that devastating. As a matter of fact, some experts say a certain amount of rejection is a good thing. The fear of being rejected seems to diminish, because we realize it wasn't so bad after all. Don't worry about your image so much. Some people are so afraid of what they are going to look like after a rejection. They are afraid of looking like they were desperate. Plus the sheer fact that they were so afraid of being rejected makes them settle for so much less than that which they can attain.

The way to overcome such fears is to take charge of them. Take that risk; break free of your fears. You will see that you really can get what you want. Don't worry about it. Then, take some time out to think about it. Think, what is the percentage of failure regarding the possibility of rejection. Think, well, what is the worst thing that can happen to me if I try it. This way you can examine what might happen in a more realistic manner.

Tell yourself you are going to do this, no matter what. Tell yourself you are going to worry and deal with whatever happens sometime later, but right now you are going to go through with it. Use your energies for what is going on right now. Don't use your energies for what might happen in the future. Stick with what is happening right now.

Stick with the book's outline strictly, without deviating from it for a while. Make up your mind and stay with it.

I SEE RED

I can remember a time when I knew this beautiful redhead whose name was Judy. She used to come into a club I worked in.

Now I told you I used to work with guys who had plastic surgery done on their faces. Most of the guys I worked with had their nose fixed, and they were what a woman would consider "very good looking." So two of these guys I worked with wanted Judy. First Dan tried his best shot and she wouldn't go out with him. With his looks, he never had much trouble with good looking women. But Judy turned him down. Then Billy, the other bartender, tried his luck with Judy. He was a good looking guy, who usually didn't have much trouble getting good looking women either. Judy turned him down too. These were regular guys; easy to get along with.

I thought about this for a while. Why didn't Judy want either one of these two good looking guys? Well, I decided to try it for myself. In the face of a very high probability of being rejected, I decided to go for it. I figured she already rejected two good looking buddies of mine, and I had never seen her with a boyfriend, so it really looked like I was walking into a flat rejection. Then I thought, what do I have to lose. I had never really worried about being rejected before, besides, who is going to laugh at me? Not my two buddies, that's for sure.

Because I had a high tolerance for rejection, I approached her with my usual confident style and technique. It turned out that she was holding out for me, because she felt that I had a unique personality that suited her. I would have never known this, and been a loser in this situation, had I not approached her.

CONQUER THE FEAR

Conquering the fear of rejection can enrich your life enormously in ways you would never imagine. Not only in your love life, but in your career as well.

A lot of people with low self-esteem, feel that they are no good at anything, and that is why they have been turned down. Or they think that they are a total failure. Or even a horrible person. If you are having feelings like these, try to rationalize to yourself that this is a problem that stems from childhood. It really is not your fault that you are having these feelings. It is more than likely your parents' fault for causing your low self-esteem.

OPTIMISM VS. PESSIMISM

So tell yourself that these feelings are not going to stop you from achieving your goal. They are not based on anything that is true or real about yourself. Don't let your whole life be ruined by these unrealistic feelings. Overpower them. Use the strong part of your mind to crush those thoughts and achieve your goal. Start to look at life in a more optimistic way. Use positive thoughts as your guide. Optimistic people achieve more in life than pessimistic people do.

Pessimistic people let negative thoughts rule their lives. If their minds tell them they are no good and will fail at what they would like to do, they simply do not try at all. They will sit back and watch the world get what it wants, while they get nothing.

TAKE CONTROL

Give the techniques in this book a chance. Most of us are highly sensitive to being rejected by a female. This is an extremely sensitive area in a man. We are more vulnerable to this than most anything else. It is one of our psychological weak points. Walking up to a beautiful woman who is a total stranger, and being turned down, is devastating for a guy.

It is like the guy who has to give a speech in front of a thousand people. He just doesn't go out there unprepared and hope he will give a great speech. No, that would be a disaster. He would look like a fool up there. He writes the speech and practices it over and over, until he knows exactly what he is going to say.

All of these anxieties and fears are under control. That is exactly how you are going to be, in control. In control of your anxieties, fears, and the situation in general. Being in control alleviates most fears in people. This book puts you in the drivers seat because you will know exactly the right things to do in these situations. So when you approach this beautiful, strange woman, you will be in the power position. The one in the power position has the confidence to achieve his goal.

Once you master the techniques, the women you approach will sense that you have many options. This will attract them even more, because you will not be projecting a desperate, subliminal message. This gives the female the feeling that you are quite at ease and are not likely to push the situation.

It can be compared to asking your boss for a raise. If he thinks that you don't have any options, you can forget about your raise. But, if he thinks you have many job offers, right away, he is willing to give you what you want.

Most of us take our rejection, and the pain it brings, and try to deal with it the best way we can. A lot of times we beat ourselves over the head after a rejection, and it really had nothing to do with us at all.

TALL JOANIE

I remember this gorgeous woman, Joanie, who used to come into a club I worked. She was a tall woman, with a great body. She was always with a big guy with long, dark hair. After they broke up, and I had some time, I decided to go out with her. I had never considered rejection very much in my life, but she told me she couldn't go out with me right now. I thought, okay. The next time I saw her, she was with another big guy with long, dark hair. He almost looked like a clone of her first boyfriend. I decided to pursue this rejection a little further. One night, when her boyfriend wasn't there, I asked her what the problem was with going out with me. I found out that she was attracted to a certain type of man. It was true. She would seek out only a type of guy that she had in her mind and closed out any other type of man. I found this to be true of certain other women also.

Sticking to my persistence, and with little regard for rejection, I decided to press the issue. I told her it was time she broke with tradition. She was limiting herself, and broadening her choices would make her a lot happier and more satisfied. I told her that these big guys rely on their size too much. She should try shorter guys who rely on ability instead. So she decided to give me her phone number, but by then I never had time to use it. We probably would have had a good time together.

The point is, I was being rejected for a reason that was beyond my control. Had I accepted the rejection and beat myself over the head, I would have never known it was simply because she was stuck on a certain type of man. All that it took to overcome the rejection, was a little of the art of persuasion.

SUMMING IT ALL UP

A lot of us say, "I have been rejected because 'I'm no good.'" And we honestly believe that. We go through life thinking there is something wrong with us. But the real facts are that we simply did not know the secrets of changing rejection, or the fear of rejection, into acceptance. So forget everything you ever learned, or thought about, rejection. Forget every rejection you ever faced in your life. Today is a new day with new knowledge. Today you have a new understanding. Today you have my over twenty years experience of finding out how it all works. Thank God you don't have to put that kind of time in. You now can walk up to any beautiful woman you want, and persuade her into seeing things your way.

Now the fear that rejection might ruin your day is replaced with "screw rejection, look what overcoming it can do for my nights."

Never stop trying. The more you put into something, the more you are going to get out of it.

Study the techniques of this book carefully. Forget about losing ten pounds, working out two hours a day, wearing a certain style of clothes, or how much money you have to make. Or even how many countries you should have visited to sound well traveled and important. None of those things make a bit of difference in whether or not you are going to be rejected by a beautiful woman. Go back and study the chapter on "Interviews With Two Thousand Beautiful Women" to understand the real reasons you could be rejected, and simply don't do them.

SUMMARY
&
SUPER TECHNIQUES

TOTALLY WITHIN HIS CONTROL

Everything a woman wants and needs and desires in the dating arena is totally within every mans control. He can get a date with a beautiful, intelligent woman, once he reads this book and he sees, yes, there are certain things about his personality he may have to modify a little bit. Yes, there are things about the way he looks he may have to modify a little bit. Yes, there are things about the way he approaches and behaves towards women that he may have to modify a little bit, but it is still totally within his control to modify these things and become everything she wants, needs and desires.

THE OBJECT OF OUR SEX DRIVE

Have you ever heard the expression, "I can't handle the bar scene" or "I can't take the dating scene today"? Well, on one hand men are saying that women are being cold and snobbish to them, yet on the other hand they are giving the women no alternative but to be cold and snobbish because of the way they approach them and because of the way they behave towards them. For example, when a man walks up to a woman and says something like, "haven't I seen you someplace before?" Well, she's heard this line a thousand times. Her mother heard it and her grandmother heard it and I can bet Wilma Flintstone heard that line a hundred thousand years ago. One of the questions that I asked on the survey I took was, What is the worst thing a man could say to you when he first approaches you? Of the 2000 women I surveyed, among other things, the number one answer for that questions was "these old lines." They are sick of hearing these old lines. Half of them are plain silly and the other half have a sexual connotation. By the way, the worst thing you can do when you first approach a woman is mention anything sexual to her. They are not out there to be the object of our sex drives. They are out there looking for relationships with men. Men are usually limited to this one line approach, or else they have this other approach (if it is a nighclub, lounge or restaurant) where they walk up to a woman and say, "Would you like to dance with me?" If she does not particularly feel like dancing at the moment, she will turn to the gentleman and say, "No, thank you." She will then go back and resume the conversation that she was having. What do you do in a situation like that? Where do you go from there? These are antiquated techniques. We learned these techniques when we were juveniles in High School. We would go to the High School dance with a few of our buddies, we walk up to the girl and say, "Hi, would you like to dance?" If she said yes, great! But if she said no, we felt like Count Dracula did after they drove a stake through his heart. We now have to walk back to our buddies who are laughing at us. We are still trying to use these juvenile approaches on the sophisticated, intelligent modern woman of today. It is not working and no one has taught these guys techniques that actually work. That's why this book is important. It is an instructional manual to teach men the techniques of how to approach women properly.

MEN HAVE "EYEGASMS" AND WOMEN HAVE "EARGASMS"

Men and women are hard wired to be different from birth. When a man sees a beautiful woman, he thinks in his mind, "well, if that was me, I wouldn't even look at someone who wasn't just as attractive." But that is how we do things as men. It is not how women do things. When we try to second guess what a woman is thinking, that is where we make our mistake. They have deeper needs, wants and feelings they want fulfilled by a man. They don't have the superficial need for a gorgeous man as we would think they do. Men have what I call "eyegasms" and women have what I call "eargasms." Every guy who reads this book can relate to the fact that if a woman is beautiful, sexy or attractive - we want it. We will act on that alone. That is all we ever needed to act. That is the way men have been hard wired. But that is not how women do things. There was a study conducted where they had a room full of men. They asked a group of women to pick out the men that they felt were attractive. They did. Then the women actually met the men. After they met and talked to the men for awhile, the women were again asked to pick out the men that they felt were attractive. The women picked out a completely different set of men this time. They picked out average guys who had personality attributes like friendly, nice personality, honest and altruistic. What I mean by altruistic is not being selfish, putting other people in front of themselves, etc. The women liked the guys who looked into their eyes and got in touch with their well being. This is what turns women on. This is what they were attracted to. The good looking guys in the room, that the women originally picked as being attractive, actually turned them off if they were full of themselves or self centered. So, you have a choice. You can be an average guy and learn to be attractive to women or you can be a gorgeous guy and turn women off. The choice is in your hands. Basically, in all the studies that have been taken, 90 percent of the women surveyed stated that looks had nothing to do with whether they were attracted to a man or not.

THE NUMBER ONE TECHNIQUE

One of the questions asked on the survey I took was, "What is the best thing a man could say to you when he first approaches you that would make you feel good and want to respond to him?" And of the 2000 women I surveyed, the number one answer for that question was, "A sincere compliment." Remember the operative word here is sincere. It takes women sometimes hours to get ready and they made it plain to me that they expected a man to be intelligent enough to appreciate that fact. The times that men have approached them as gentlemen, and paid them a sincere compliment, meant something to them. They never forgot it. That is what I was trying to dig down to find out. I wanted to develop a system and a technique for men so I could alleviate this anxiety that men have when they are approaching women today. I wanted men to know they were doing exactly the right thing. For example, if a man sees a woman at the shore, in the mall, on the street or at work, he should approach her by saying one of the top ten opening pick up lines I have in this book. Simply walk up to her and say "Excuse me, it's never easy meeting a complete stranger, especially one as beautiful as you, without being properly introduced, but shall we try anyway?" You then extend out your hand, and say, "My name is 'so and so', and you are?" And she will tell you her name. You can replace the word beautiful with lovely. You can replace the word beautiful with pretty. As long as you say it as sincerely as possible. If she really looks beautiful to you, then say "beautiful." If she really looks lovely to you, then say "lovely." You can replace the word "beautiful" with "lovely" or "pretty" in any of those top ten pick up lines, just make sure you are sincere. Sincerity is the key.

BUILDING A RAPPORT

Now that you have approached the woman in a proper way, everything you say and do from this point on will cause her to decide whether she wants to go out with you or not. You have to build a rapport with the woman. Pick common grounds, safe territories, establish connections, understand similarities. Women expect men to think a certain way. Creative, witty, intelligently. And men have to convey important information to the female that she will take and evaluate. He has to convey that he is an individual that is ambitious, decisive and industrious. She will then take this information and decide whether this gentleman is going to rise to the top of his field someday. It gives her clues to his future. Women pick the most resourceful men. They always have all through history. Go all the way back to Fred Flintstone. Wilma picked Fred Flintstone because he knew how to build a fire, hunt and move boulders around. She wasn't looking for a loser then just as the women of our time are not looking for losers today. Basically, all of women's preferences through evolution have now become instinct. It is instinctive for her to pick a resourceful man. Don't worry, it is not that stressful. No man has to be a loser. As long as you have a job with a future, and you convey to her that you are the type of individual who is going after that future, that is the key. You may elaborate on your job title to make it look more appealing just as anyone would do on a resume to make it look impressive. You must embellish a little - show your potential. Make the truth sound good. Let's say you hired a professional to put together your resume. When it was completed, you wouldn't recognize the person on the resume. Believe it or not, that's you. This is because the professional knows how to embellish and show your potential so that you will get that job. This is the same technique you must learn when talking to a woman so that you can get that date. Let's say you're a garbage man, and, by the way, there is nothing wrong with being a garbage man. Don't tell her that you are the executive producer at Warner Brothers Studios. You're going a little over the top now. Stay within your ballpark. Tell her you are a Sanitation Engineer who is up for that "EXECUTIVE" sanitation position. I am being facetious but I hope you are starting to get my drift.

WHAT TURNS HER OFF

One of the questions I asked on the survey I took was, "What turns you off about a man in a situation like this?" From the 2000 women I surveyed, I got so much information about that one particular question that I had to make 14 categories. You may go back and review it but I will give you a couple of examples now. One of the main turn offs was when a man is "full of himself." This is when you are telling her how wonderful and great you think you are. There is a fine line between intelligently describing where you are heading in the future and boasting about how great you think you are. You have to learn where that fine line is. Also, don't badger her with questions. When a man badgers a woman with questions, she feels like you're throwing hardballs at her and that she has to hit back a home run every time. This puts a lot of stress on a very delicate situation.

HOT BUTTONS

It is always good to be pressing on hot buttons when you approach a woman. One of them is being super neat and clean. Have you ever heard the expression "A woman can't resist a man in uniform?" Well, you are pushing on that same hot button when you show up super neat and clean from the top of your head down to the tip of your toes - right down to your fingernails. Women have razor eyes for cleanness and details. It's a function in their minds that women have developed through evolution. If a man and a woman meet and a few minutes later you asked the man to describe the woman, he will not be able to give you that many details. However, if you ask the woman to describe the man, she will do it right down to the last detail. Men have developed different functions throughout evolution, but they are for a bigger design. The great outdoors, building bridges, football, etc., but not for details.

STANDUP COMIC

Having a sense of humor is a hot button. It is very important. I have read all there is to read about sense of humor and interviewed 2000 women on the subject. I have learned that women today will not stampede over Tom Cruise to get to Buddy Hacket. If you are a hunchback, all the knock-knock jokes in the world aren't going to get you anywhere. And unless your name is Jim Carey, please keep the asparagus out of your nose when you take her to dinner. The last thing you want to do is be a standup comic. You are actually turning her off this way. The last thing you want to do is tell her a joke. If the joke is funny, she will laugh. If the joke is not funny, she will nervously laugh a little bit. Either way, you have just stalled the conversation. You've reached a dead end. That is something you don't want to do. What I mean by sense of humor is take something you have read or learned recently that is humorous and incorporate it into the conversation. This should make her laugh a little. The secret is to keep the flow of the conversation moving.

GETTING THE DATE

There are a few things you will have to consider when asking her for her a date. Don't always expect the woman to give you an intimate five hour Friday or Saturday night date right after you have met her. It is usually too big of a commitment. It is advisable to move slowly. Consider asking her for a simple luncheon date for a number of reasons. She'll feel it will only take an hour of her time which is more agreeable to her and for you (believe it or not). Both of you will feel that you are not stuck 5 hours together if things are not working out well. Remember, women are vulnerable and you want to make it as safe a situation as possible for her. Let her pick the meeting place. It could be right around the corner from where she works in a bright and airy restaurant where there are lots of people around. A place where she feels safe and comfortable.

THE SUPER TECHNIQUE

This technique will get you her phone number every single time (if you've done everything I have told you up to now). After you've had your conversation it is now time to ask for that date. You will say, "It was lovely talking to you and I know you must go now, but before you go, this is what I'd like to do." You will take out your business card or piece of paper, put your phone number on it and hand it to her and say "Let's exchange numbers. If you give me your work number, I will send roses to your office the day I call you for a lunch date. If you take my call, we will go out and have a wonderful and enjoyable lunch together. If you do not take the call, I will understand completely and never bother you again." This makes it a win/win situation for her. She knows she can't lose. Either way she is going to get something that she wants. This is a deep psychological point that I want you to understand. She will give you her phone number, guaranteed. When the roses arrive at her workplace all the other girls at the office will say, "who sent you those roses? Who is this guy? I want to meet a guy like this. Where did you meet such a romantic guy? You have to go out with him, he must be wonderful." Believe me, the day you send her roses her heart will melt, and she will definitely take your call, guaranteed. By the way, you don't have to send her a dozen roses, that could be a little expensive. You could send just one rose, if the florist arranges it tastefully. And, for a few dollars, you could have a date with the beautiful girl of your dreams.

THE SUPER "PUPPY" TECHNIQUE

This technique is truly super, although it does require one small carnivorous mammal. That's right you're going to need a puppy. I don't care how you get one. Buy one, rent one, borrow one from a friend, just get your hands on one. You will only need it for a few days at the most. Take your newly acquired puppy to the busiest street in town or on your college campus or even to the beach and watch the magic begin. This little puppy will give you instant appeal with every woman you encounter. Women adore little puppies and adore men who seem to have compassion for these little creatures. Women will feel an instantaneous connection to your delightful little furry animal. When you see a woman who has spotted your puppy, immediately say, "would you like to pet him?" As a matter of fact, most of the time they will approach you and ask what your puppy's name is, how old he is, what kind of a puppy he is, how long have you had him, etc. All questions that will lead to an open discussion. A woman will open up in this non-threatening situation giving you an opportunity to get to know her and acquire her phone number. This super technique is a sure bet for anyone. The only problem with borrowing a puppy is, when you do get a date and the woman wants to see the dog, you'll have to tell her you were just "puppy sitting" for a couple of weeks while your friend was on vacation. By the way, talking parrots and babies make wonderful puppy substitutes. If, for instance, your sister has a baby and allows you to baby sit for the day, use the same technique, you'll get the same response. (Just make sure you tell them it's you sister's baby and not yours.)

THE SUPER PARTY TECHNIQUE

Here's a technique that you can use that actually happened to me through a string of coincidental events. What you do with this technique is entirely up to you. I am merely going to reiterate the exact course of events that lead up to getting so many phone numbers from beautiful women. A number of years ago, myself and a few other gentlemen were hired to petition beautiful women and request that they come to an elaborate party where there would be plenty of food and drink, and many known celebrities. In other words, this company wanted to "dress up" the party with beautiful women. We were commissioned to seek out beautiful women anywhere we could (ie: nightclubs, restaurants, malls, boardwalk, etc.) and inform them that there was going to be a big party with lots of celebrities, and that they were invited unconditionally. The beautiful girls that I solicited were told the particulars about the party. I told them that they could bring up to three girlfriends or even their boyfriends, if they preferred. I also told them of the many celebrities they'd probably rub elbows with. I told them it would cost them absolutely nothing. This totally made it a win-win situation for these women. The only detail missing about the party was the exact date, which hadn't been established yet. I asked unpretentiously for their phone numbers so that I could inform them of the exact date of the party. In the course of a month's time, I had approximately 100 phone numbers from women who were interested in attending such a party. To my surprise, the organizers of the party were never able to follow through and complete the project. After contemplating the course of events, I realized that I had in my possession approximately 100 phone numbers of beautiful women whom I had talked to and gotten to know a little bit. I thought I should call them back and tell them of the failed party attempt. I did, and while we were talking on the phone I decided to ask if they would consider going out on a date with me. To my surprise, the majority of the women agreed. I now had about 70 beautiful women agreeing to go out with me. Whether you use this technique or not for acquiring phone numbers from beautiful women is entirely up to you.

You could actually do something similar to this technique, but it's results are not as powerful. Contact the owners of a new nightclub that is being built or just opening in your area. Most of the time, they'll give you 100 free passes to distribute among perspective customers, plus you will be compensated for your time. You, in turn, would give every beautiful woman you see a free pass to the new club. This gives you an opportunity to approach a beautiful woman, promote the new club for the owners, and get to know this girl. During the course of your conversation, you can tell her that you will be at the club Friday and Saturday night and looking forward to seeing her there. Now you have established a rapport and broken the ice with 100 women to whom you have distributed passes. When you see them at the club, you will already know their names and be able to approach them comfortably.

TIC-TAC-TOE

This technique is for the super shy individual who cannot bring himself to approach a beautiful woman. If you happen to be in a nightclub, restaurant, or a coffee shop, and there is a beautiful woman sitting there, try to obtain an available seat next to her. All you need is a pen and a small piece of paper, even a small napkin will do. Draw the outline of a tic-tac-toe board on your paper. Put an "O" in the middle of the tic-tac-toe board and simply slide the pen and paper, with the tic-tac-toe board on it, over to her. It's obvious you're inviting her to play a simple game. She will put an "X" in one of the boxes and slide the paper pack to you. Continue until you get up enough nerve to say, "Hi," and start your conversation. It has been known to take up to two or three games before a conversation actually breaks out.

CROSSWORD PUZZLE

This technique requires a pen and the purchase of the local newspaper for a few cents. It is the same scenario as before. Try to spot a beautiful girl sitting in a coffee house, donut shop, restaurant, or outdoor cafe. Have the paper opened up to the crossword puzzle. Pick one of the easiest questions on the crossword puzzle. An example would be, a five letter word for "big body of water," which is "OCEAN." Now ask the girl if she wouldn't mind helping you with a simple request. Tell her you are stuck on a crossword question. She'll probably say something like, "Okay, I'll try." You don't want to make her look stupid by asking her a hard question. This would negate the whole process. She'll probably know the answer to the easy question, and feel good about it. Your response will be, "Of course, why didn't I see that? Thanks, you seem good at this," and start your conversation from there.

As an added thought, you may want to inform her that you do crossword puzzles every day to help increase your vocabulary, which is important to the type of career you are pursuing.

PERSONAL ITEM

One can create a powerful bond with a complete stranger, or in your case a beautiful women, with a simple request. This technique is based on a study done many years ago. All you need for this technique is a simple personal item. A small radio was used when they first conducted the study. I prefer the personal item to be a pair of gloves, a hat, a newspaper, or a combination of all three. Simply place the personal item down in front of you. It may be at a bar, a coffee shop, or again an outside cafe. Tell the beautiful woman that you will be right back, you just want to wash your hands in the men's room for a minute. Ask her if she wouldn't mind watching your hat (or other personal item) until you return. The power of a "positive situational bond" has just been formed between you and this person. When this study was originally conducted, they had a third person try to *take* the personal item. The individual who was asked to watch the personal item actually chased the third person down the street to retrieve it. Now, you're going to use this powerful bond to your advantage. When you return, you will thank this beautiful girl and offer her a small token of your appreciation by buying her a cup of coffee, or whatever seems appropriate. Use this opportunity you've created to start a conversation which will eventually lead to a phone number.

EXCITEMENT

Don't wait for somebody to bring excitement into your life. I want you to be a person who takes the initiative. Bring excitement into someone else's life. When you are ready for that date beyond the initial ½ hour lunch date we discussed earlier, don't ask her out to dinner and a movie, be a little more creative. Instead of a movie, tell her you would like to take her to a live play or live TV show. Instead of telling her you would like to take her to the shore, tell her you would like to rent a couple of jet skis this weekend with her. The idea is to bring excitement into her life. Think up something exciting to do on a date. Women are looking for excitement and you are going to be that person to give it to her.

JUGGLING ACT

Getting a date with a beautiful woman is almost like a juggling act. You have to utilize all of these techniques that you have learned so far. It is like spinning plates on sticks, you have to keep all the plates spinning. You have to approach her properly, be super neat and clean, have a sense of humor, etc. You can do everything I have taught you, yet, if you show up with dirty finger nails or disheveled in any way, the plates start falling down. There is an art to everything in this life. Be sure to master the art of all these techniques that you have learned, and you will have more beautiful women than you can handle, guaranteed.

QUESTIONS & ANSWERS

Q. ***I would really like to impress a woman on the first date. Where can I take her that would knock her socks off and make her want to go out with me again?***

A. I advise men to take the initiative when dating. Don't wait for someone to bring excitement into your life, be the one who brings excitement into someone else's. All my work is based on deep psychological points. Let me explain this in the simplest way I know how. There have been many studies done on human emotion. One by *Schachter and Singer's* called the *Two Factor Theory*, now stay with me here because it gets interesting. According to this theory, emotion-provoking events produce increased arousal in human beings. In response to feelings of arousal, we human beings search the external environment in order to identify the causes of our feelings. The factors we then select play a key role in determining the label we place on our arousal. In others words, we have to identify the cause of our arousal and label it. Maybe an example here would make it clear. A field study was done in 1994. A situation was arranged so that female hikers would encounter a male research assistant, either on solid ground or while crossing a swaying suspension bridge high above a rocky gorge. Later, the researchers asked the women to rate their attraction to the assistant. According to the theory, the women who met the assistant on a swaying bridge would report finding him more attractive than those who met him on solid ground. Believe it or not, this is precisely what they found. In fact, not only did the female hikers who met him on the bridge rate him as more attractive, they were more likely to want to call him for a date. Findings such as these suggest that the Schachter-Singer theory provides important insights into the process through which we label our own emotions. Now, getting back to your question, if you want the woman you are taking out to find you extremely attractive, and want to date you again, then you should find something exciting to do on your date. Take her to an amusement park where there are roller coaster rides. The excitement she will experience sitting next to you on the roller coaster ride will be converted into feelings of attraction towards you. The same hormones that are released from a lustful kiss are exactly the same as when we are frightened on a roller coaster ride. The adrenal gland produces adrenaline, nor-adrenaline, and testosterone at that time. Women also produce testosterone from their ovaries, exactly the same way whether it be from a kiss or an exciting ride. It's quite possible that she will mistake the thrill of being frightened for lust for you. Take her ski-diving, river rafting, on a helicopter ride over the city at night, anything other than a boring dinner followed by a boring movie. Use your imagination. Take her skiing or to a haunted house or even to a scary movie. Try something exciting. Just make sure that both of you will be pretty much still alive when you're done!

Q. ***I've heard that the "bad boy" image appeals to women. Should I change my image and become this "bad boy" that all the girls want?***

A. In the past, many researchers have attempted to discover exactly what types of men, women consider most desirable for relationship partners. Harold, ES and Milhausen, RR at the Department of Human Relations at the University of Guelph, Ontario, Canada investigated thousands of university women on their perceptions of "nice guys." This research tried to focus in on specifically whether women perceived nice guys to be more or less sexually successful than guys who were considered "not nice." They tried to analyze women's interpretations of the "nice guy" label. More than half of the women agreed that nice guys have fewer sexual partners, however, a big majority of the women also reported a preference for a "nice guy" over a "bad boy" as a date. They also found out that women in general who placed a lesser emphasis on the importance of sex, who had fewer sexual partners, and who were less accepting of men who had many sexual partners, were more likely to choose the nice guy as a dating partner. In general, the findings of this study indicated that nice guys are probably more likely to have fewer sexual partners but are highly desired by women for committed relationships. So, if one is to analyze this study of the "nice guy" stereotype, then it is clear that women prefer nice guys over bad boys. Although women believe that bad boys are having more sex, the truth is, none of them wanted to date a bad boy. So, where are all these bad boys getting their sex from? One would have to surmise that the bad boys are getting their sex from the bad girls. Either way, it seems the "bad boys" will only attract a minority of the female population. You know who I mean, the bimbos.

Q. ***I have a big problem talking to girls. I don't know what to talk about. To sit down and have a conversation with a girl would be just about out of the question, let alone ask her out on a date. Give me some guidelines to follow to help me out with this problem.***

A. Having a conversation with a woman and having a conversation with a man are almost two completely different things. Starting at the age of two years old, boys and girls tend to gravitate toward their own gender. Boys play guns with other boys. As we grow up our best friends are boys, we hang out with boys, play sports with boys. By the time we reach puberty and the dating age, we basically have never communicated with the opposite sex. Unbeknownst to us, girls have been communicating by sharing their feelings and emotions all this time. Part of the problem here is that men are "topic" and "fact oriented," that is how we converse with other men. That is the language we speak. Women, on the other hand, are less direct and more circuitous. They can actually say one thing and mean another. Men's conversations tend to focus on preserving their independence. On the other hand, the woman's language promotes more familiarity, more informal warmth. So, with that in mind, talk about the school you go to, movies, T.V. shows, the last trip you took, and those sorts of things. Try to show a friendly, casual interest in her as a human being. You can state your opinion on certain subjects and ask her about her opinion on the same subjects. Try to volley the conversation back and forth, keeping it basically simple. Find a subject you both have in common and you both enjoy. If she is a receptive individual, she will respond by revealing something about herself or her opinion on the subject you are talking about. During your conversation you have to make a connection with her. Find out what hobbies, interests, skills, or activities she may have that you might have in common, and connect with her on that level. For example, you may both shop at the same mall, you may both go to the same school or university, you may be studying the same courses, or perhaps you may go to the same church or synagogue. Your rapport should always be friendly, gentle, and non-threatening. Reveal something about yourself, perhaps your name and some opinions you may have on certain subjects. Ask her what her take is on the situation. Then try to volley it back and forth. Also ask yourself where are these women who like to do these things and where do they do them? Now go to those functions and you will have a lot in common with the women that are there. As you have learned in the Summary of this book, women have revealed that there is a deeper message they are listening for during your conversation. If your intent, by having a conversation with this woman, is to get a date with her, then you must go one step further. You will have to convey certain information during your conversation to this woman that she will evaluate. You must convey that you are the type of person that is ambitious (one who is goal oriented), decisive (able to make good decisions), and industrious (one who is not confined to his peripheries). She will take this information and come to some conclusions about your future potential. It gives her clues to where you are going in life. Women pick the most resourceful men with the brightest futures. This is what prompts a woman to say "YES" when a man asks for a date.

Q. I am a guy that is 5 feet 4 inches tall. We all know women are not attracted to small men. What can you do to help me?

A. You are not alone with this problem. They even did a study where they had six men standing side by side. Three of the men were tall, about 6' 1" or 6' 2". The other guys were about your height. 99% of the time the women desired the tall men when they were judging on physique alone. Women have this mental image of a tall knight in shining armor coming to their rescue. Blame it on fairy tale stories and overzealous mothers. In a crowded room you are going to be the less desirable target when standing next to a man who is 6 feet tall or more. I have had to coach many short men into getting dates with beautiful girls by using my techniques. On one occasion, the great genius Howard Stern asked me to coach some of his interns, using my techniques on how to get dates. Some of these interns were short men about your size and some of these interns where husky (fat), follicley impaired (bald), men who did not have a clue when it came to getting a date with a beautiful woman. All of these interns, including the short guys, got dates with beautiful girls within one hours time. This show that I did for Howard happened to be one of his highest rated shows of all time. When this particular show aired, many other producers and editors called me to create other shows similar to this one. One in particular was *Penthouse Magazine* who was astounded by the show I did for Howard Stern and wanted to do something similar for their magazine. They asked me to meet them on the upper east side in New York City's night club scene. They gave me an individual who was approximately your height and who about 50 years old. An individual who had no physical attributes that any woman would consider attractive. My mission that night was to teach this person techniques from my book to see how well he scored. We started at 9:00pm and by midnight this little man got 5 confirmed dates and phone numbers from beautiful girls. As an added bonus, a beautiful 25 year old female accountant with long black hair and blue eyes, about 5 foot 7 was so enamored by this little man using my techniques, that she actually left and went home with him that night. She subsequently dated him for some time afterwards. You could go to my website at www.4secret.com for more information on these particular issues. Women are not going to flock toward a small man. The small men I coached were taught to take an initiative when it comes to getting what they want. They learned that one must be a go-getter. They learned that a little courage and a few good techniques is all that is needed to get what you want in this world. So, to all you short guys out there, believe in what I am saying when I tell you, do not let your height hold you back for anything that you want in this life.

Q. ***I always see beautiful girls shopping in my local grocery store. How can I meet one of these girls without looking ridiculous?***

A. We all see these beautiful girls strolling through the aisles, purchasing groceries, totally oblivious to anything else. First off, no matter where you go, be vigilant in your daily travels. Always be super neat and clean, even if you are just going to the grocery store. It is a hot button for women. You never know if the next person you meet will be your *dream girl*. I have instructed my staff to test techniques in the grocery stores for a number of years, and here are some of the results. You will need to carry a magic marker for this technique. Let's say you see a beautiful girl in the produce aisle. Grab a banana or some other type of fruit and write down "I think you're beautiful" on the fruit, and slip it into the baby seat section of her cart while she's not looking. When she notices the additional produce with writing on it, she'll pick it up and look at it, then look at you. You'll say, "I had a pen, I had some fruit, I wanted to tell you how beautiful you are. What else could I do?" The girl usually laughs. Now you have broken the ice. Introduce yourself and start your conversation.

If you see a beautiful girl standing in the cold cut section, waiting to buy lunch meat and holding her number ticket, go over and get your number ticket. Now ask her what her number is. When she gives you her ticket number, say," I wish it was that easy to get your home number." Better yet, get your ticket number first, now when a beautiful girl comes over to get her ticket number, say, "You look like you're in a hurry, let's trade tickets so you'll be next." Then you'll say, "Hi, my name is so-and-so, and your name is?" At this point keep the conversation going until you get her phone number.

A good technique is to ask the woman you are interested in for some advice on certain products. If you're in the tomato sauce aisle, ask her which is the best tomato sauce to use because you have to cook for a group of guys Friday night. Make it look like this is the first time you've had to cook on your own and you really need her advice.

Another technique is to get in line behind the girl you have your eye on and say, "you have a lot of groceries there, I'd be happy to lend a hand if you need some help." It is especially funny if she only has 1 or 2 items. If she says yes, that is a great opportunity. If she says no, it is still a good opportunity to start a conversation. We have gotten a high percent of phone numbers using these techniques in grocery stores. Try them, you have nothing to lose. Grocery stores are a great place to do a little mingling. Remember, never pass up an opportunity to met a beautiful girl no matter where you are.

Q. ***The problem is, every time I attempt to approach an attractive women, something strange happens to me. My palms get sweaty, my heart starts to pound, and I begin hyperventilating. I can't do it. How can I overcome this problem?***

A. The majority of men out there have the same problem you do, it is inescapable. It is called fear. Yours just happens to be the fear of being rejected by an attractive woman. One thing is for sure, fear is a powerful force that no one is immune to. It is part of being a human being. Fortunately for you, there are ways to overcome it. The fact that you are giving into this fear has limited your joy and your choices in life. Your fear is unhealthy because your brain perceives things to be a threat that are really not. You must develop skills that will get you what you want. Unreasonable fears, such as the one you have, can usually be traced to something in ones life experience. Maybe you have been rejected by women in the past and fear this will happen to you in the future. The idea is to recognize the first sign of fear and slow down the brains chemical response. It is not always easy. Here are some tips you may use to help overcome your fear. Make cognitive changes and learn to take charge of yourself. Try to develop positive affirmative thinking. Replace negative thoughts with positive self-nurturing thoughts. Stop fearful thoughts by short circuiting the fearful thoughts and ideas that keep fear and negativity going. Challenge irrational beliefs. Seek rational alternatives to your battle against fear. Learn the techniques of my book on approaching women in the proper way and then imagine yourself going through it, step by step. This practice will help you desensitize your fear. Now use those new skills in a practical sense by striking up a conversation with an attractive woman. Take small steps at a time. Approach the woman for a quick "hello" or a chat, the way I have outlined in my book, and then walk away. You will begin to understand that these women really did want to have a conversation with you. It is also good to learn some stress reduction techniques that include breathing exercises. If all else fails, consider psychotherapy or prescribed medications. Doctors actually have medications that are helpful in controlling fears until you have conquered them.

Q. ***My problem is, women never or very rarely give me a second date even though I practically plead for one. I'm an easy going guy and even let the woman decide what she would like to do on the date. What am I doing wrong?***

A. If you want a second date you have to do everything right on the first date. Earlier we talked about taking a woman on an exciting date. That applies here, too. These are just suggestions on how to make her feel comfortable and enjoy her date with you. I want you to create an environment that will allow both you and your date to relax, get to know one another, and have fun. Don't be such an easy going type of guy letting the woman make all the decisions on a date. From now on, I want you to have everything under control. Make sure all the bases are covered. Be sure to plan your date well. Know where you are going, know how to get there, make sure you have enough gas, know exactly what it is going to cost, and carry extra money for unforeseen expenses. The next date you go on, follow the rules I give. First off, I want you to be yourself. Let your date get to know the real you and above all be honest with her. Secondly, I want you to be a good listener. Your date will probably tell you everything you need to know about herself in the first 20 minutes. Train yourself to really hear and focus on what she is saying word for word, until she is finished talking. It sounds easy but it's actually very difficult. Listen to what your date is really saying, not what you want to hear. I always emphasize having a sense of humor. Make sure you keep a sense of humor about yourself and everything in general. Connect with your date and become totally in sync with her. Try to adopt the same speaking rhythm that your date has. If she is speaking softly, you should speak softly. Try to share the same pace with your date. If she is energized, you should be energized. Don't drink too much. You may say and do things you would not ordinarily say and do when you are sober. Don't be afraid to give freely on a date. Almost every study taken reveals that females value the financial abilities of potential mates. So, don't be afraid to spend a little money. Always compliment your date, whether it be on her beauty, her hair, or her clothes, and make sure it is sincere. Make sure you are on time. Never forget to romance your date. Romantic gestures show her that you can act from the heart. This will captivate her. Bring her flowers when you go to pick her up, candlelit dinner in a quiet restaurant, slow walks on the beach, etc., you get the idea. Remember, your date has a beginning, a middle, and an end. Pace yourself. Basically, a date is for getting to know one another, relaxing, and enjoying yourself. Don't over do it, always leave them wanting more. Try to end the date with a hug and a kiss. How long the hug lasts will usually determine what will happen next. If you hug your date and she hugs you back, and it lasts longer than a second, this is an indication that it is time to kiss her. During the hug, if she gazes into your eyes with her lips parted slightly and her head is tilted upward, this indicates she wants a kiss. Try to give her a serious kiss at this point. If your date allows this type of a kiss, you can bet she can't wait to see you again. For a woman, a great kisser is a guy who takes his time. Make it sensual more than sexual. That means no *tonsil hockey.*

Q. ***I was thinking about joining a gym and starting a workout routine. The biggest reason I want to get in shape is to attract women. Are body builders more attractive to women than non body builders?***

A. I interviewed 500 of the most beautiful women that I could find, regarding this question. I used a picture of a body builder, dressed in a pair of shorts, and a picture of a non-body builder. With a computer program I took the body builder's head and put it on both men. This gave me the same exact face on two different bodies in order to keep the study as scientific as possible. I asked the 500 women that I surveyed to answer a number of questions, strictly on a visual basis. The first question on the survey was: *Which man do you find yourself focusing most of your attention on - A, the non-body builder or B, the body* *builder, and how much time are you focusing on each.* I found that the women were focusing 99% - 100% of their time on the body builder, not paying much attention at all to the non- body builder. Next, I asked about specific body parts. Question No. 2 read: *Regarding the man you are focusing most of your attention on, what part of his anatomy is most interesting to you first?* The number one answer for that question was, the pectoral muscles or chest of the subject. When I asked what the second most interesting part of his anatomy was, the women answered *arms or biceps.* The third most interesting part of the man's anatomy to these women were the *stomach or abs.* This leads us to surmise that the chest, arms and stomach, in that order, are the most interesting parts of the body builders anatomy to a female. We got a lot of feedback about the groin area, but that is another subject entirely. They did focus their attention in that area briefly. Suffice to say that the women who took the survey were satisfied just seeing that he had some kind of normal size "package." A lot of women showed interest in wanting to see the body builder's butt, however, they were offered a frontal picture only.

Since I was interviewing women on this subject, I decided to one step further and ask, *Do you feel that the body builder would produce healthier children, and does it matter?* When studies like these were first introduced many years ago, women would have given the appropriate answer. However, the women of the millennium are answering questions, not with the *appropriate answers* anymore, but with their true feelings. A staggering majority of the women responded to this question by stating, *Who cares, I would just like to find out how he makes children.* This sheds a completely different light on how women have answered questions in the past and how they answer them today. So, in answer to your question, yes, body building will definitely give you the edge. When comparing body builders to non-body builders, women in general will clearly focus their attention on the body builder. If one of your reasons for getting into body building is to attract women, then I can clearly state, strictly on a visual basis, the body builder has it over the average guy, hands down.

Q. ***Give me some advice on how to get this girl that sits beside me in my business class at the University. I lack confidence and fear rejection and I'm not very good at this. I am certainly not going to get her attention with my looks. What is your advice?***

A. First of all, you don't have to be too aggressively in this situation. Because she's in your class or, in your case, sitting beside you, it is a great opportunity for you to get to know her as a person first. You have nothing but time. Never test the depth of the water with both feet. I don't want you to ask her out right away, she may say "no" and you'll both feel awkward sitting next to each other for the rest of the semester. Having a plan is crucial. Stay loose, keep your relationship with her light, flexible, and open. You both have a lot in common, ie: class assignments, your teacher, and maybe even your careers in life. Use this to your advantage. The best recommendation I can give you in a situation like this is to ask her for some friendly advise on a class project. Most women are usually more than willing to help out. Take advantage of that tendency. Admit to her that you don't normally do this, but you are going to ignore your usual shyness in this particular case.

The next time class is over, synchronize your timing so that you are right behind or in front of her when you leave the classroom and say, "I didn't understand the instructions for the last assignment, do you have a moment to explain it to me?" I want you to build a friendship and bond with her at first by discussing class projects. You could also connect with her by discussing whether or not you like the professor and whatever else you may have in common. By building a personal friendship with her you could find out whether or not she has a steady boyfriend. The closer you two become, the better your chances will be for getting a date. Always be charming towards her during the conversation. Subtly compliment her on her hair, eyes, or smile in a sincere and honest way. Once you establish a friendship with her, and determine there is no steady boyfriend, you have overcome most of your obstacles.

Remember, we all must face rejection in our lifetime. It's a perfectly natural thing. The question is, are you going to let it stop you? You and I and every other guy out there has to face the nervousness and the sweaty palms that is associated with asking a woman out. Remember, it is just one date with one girl and it is not the end of the world. No guts, no glory. Life's a risk or it is nothing at all. When the time comes, don't appear too eager, too desperate, or too tense. Simply ask her if she would like to join you for a cup of coffee between classes. This is a good starting point. By this time, if you have made a legitimate connection with her as a friend, there should be no problem.

Q. I thought I knew everything about body language, but when I try to use it in a practical sense, it always seems to backfire. I think a woman is interested in me from her

body language, but it usually turns out that I'm wrong. What's going on here? What am I doing wrong?

A. Review Chapter 3 one more time to refresh your memory. Human beings communicate with each other in many ways. We do it with body postures, eye contact, facial expressions, and touching as well as through speech. Body language is a complex system of interpersonal interactions. The knowledge of body language increases our perception and is usually one more instrument of improving your chances for a date. A lot of the body language that you perceive as positive from women may be very misleading. According to a new study at Vienna's Ludwig Boltzmann Institute of Urban Ethology, 50 male-female pairs of strangers, who thought they were asked to rate videos in a particular room, suddenly and unexpectedly found themselves alone with each other, when the person conducting the experiment excused them self and left the room. For a certain period of time, the 50 male-female pairs were secretly recorded and then examined for women's "courtship" or "body language" signals, ie: eye contact, hair tossing, stroking the palms, thighs, or wrists, hair flipping, etc. "Rejection" signals were also measured for both parties. Rejection signals, such as avoiding conversations, were also measured along with exactly how long each person took to speak. After the study, each participant was asked to rate how attractive the others were to them and their own interest level in dating that person. According to the study's author, Karl Grammer, Ph.D., "women surprisingly do not send clear rejection signals. Women also will send sexually explicit signals without having much interest in the man." This may be the catch 22 dilemma that you find yourself caught up in. When women are sending out these sexually explicit

...s, men believe it's time to approach them and start ...vealing everything about themselves, allowing women to verify their initial impressions. Their findings showed, for example, that women used subtle signals such as nodding in agreement to direct the flow of conversation. Most importantly, the study found that women will actually avoid contact with men who talked too much initially. It appears there is more to body language than meets the eye. I would suggest that you do not reveal everything about yourself upon your initial contact, and that would apply to any guy. One should ask open ended questions and show casual interest in her as a human being. Try to connect with her on whatever interests, hobbies, or activities you both may have in common. Then simply close your mouth and listen!

Q. ***Where are the best places to meet available women? Most women I see are just too busy in their every day lives to be bothered with a strange guy walking up to them and asking for a date.***

A. I have done many talk shows with regard to this book. One day I was a guest on the Sally Jessy Raphael show and an audience member asked me "Where is a good place to meet women?" I got up out of my seat, walked down to the women that were in his vicinity, and asked them whether they were single and available. The first one said, "No, I'm married." I asked the second one the same question and she said, "I Could be, if the right guy comes along." I asked the third girl, and she reluctantly said, "yes." Remember, we were taping a show at the time, and people were a little more reserved than usual. I asked several other girls in his vicinity if they were available and they said, "yes." I asked the girls, who claimed they were available, if they wouldn't mind meeting a nice guy right now. They said, "sure, why not." I showed the man the proper way to introduce himself to the girls that were single and available. (Review Chapter 6) He did introduce himself, and I said, "There, you just met several beautiful girls." I then announced to him and the audience, "There is no one place that women go for 45 minutes per day to meet men." I turned to the gentleman and said, "You are allowed to meet women anyplace at anytime." The audience, who were predominantly women, applauded in approval. (You can review that video at my website, www.4secret.com. Press the video button next to Sally Jessy Raphael's name.) The point is, no matter where you are or what you are doing, you have the right to approach and have a conversation with a woman you are attracted to, as long as you are a gentleman and do it in a sincere and proper manner.

There are many other possibilities that you can investigate. According to the publication, *Sex in America*, over 60% of married couples were introduced to each other though mutual friends, a family member, coworker, classmate, or next door neighbor. Make sure you get the word out to these people. Let them become aware of the fact that you are interested in meeting an attractive woman to date. Tell them that you would appreciate an introduction to single woman they may know. Of the people who are going out together right now, 50% of them met through a mutual friend or the like. Here are some possibilities you want to consider. If you are in school, meet someone right in your class. The next social function you are invited to, be it wedding or bar mitzvah, make sure you go and mingle. Try this technique the next time you

... vacation. Go to the hotel lounge and send a drink ...r to a prospective single girl at the bar or at a table. You don't even have to talk to her that night. I guarantee you will see her again at pool side or at the beach the next day. Walk up to her and say, "Hi, my name is so-and-so. I'm the guy who bought you the drink last night. I didn't come over then because I thought you might be waiting for your escort." She'll say, "No, I wasn't waiting for anyone, you should have come over to say hello." Voila! You're on your way. Another great idea is to go out and join clubs that are related to the activities, hobbies, and sports that you are normally interested in. You will find women there that have the same interest. Believe it or not, your synagogue or church is a good place to meet women. According to statistics, over 75% of married couples have a similar religious background. The whole idea here is to get out there into the real world and interact with as many women as possible. Remember, Hear no women, see no women,...***feel no women***!